Pressing on...
when you'd rather
Press Stop!

By

Leland W. Streck

Published by
RAS House
Milbank, South Dakota
2001

Copyright 2001
Leland W. Streck

All rights reserved. No part of this book may be reproduced in any form, except for the inclusion of brief quotations in a review, without permission in writing from the author or publisher.

Scripture taken from the NEW AMERICAN STANDARD BIBLE , Copyright 1960, 1962, 1963, 1968, 1971, 1972, 1973, 1975, 1977, 1995 by the Lockman Foundation. Used by permission.

Library of Congress Control Number: 2001126446

ISBN: 0-9708899-0-9

First Printing   2001

Additional copies of this book are available by mail.
Send $15.00 each (includes tax and postage) to:
Leland W. Streck
412 S. 4th St.
Milbank, SD 57252
(605) 432-9050

Printed in the U.S.A. by
Morris Publishing
3212 East Highway 30
Kearney, NE 68847
1-800-650-7888

Acknowledgments

We would like to acknowledge the following people for their input and ministry in our lives in some form in the completion of this book.

For their help during Ryan's life: Drew, Lin, Mike, Bob, Dr. Provine, Denise, Dawn, Chad, Margie, Ted, Pam, Terry, Barry, Tommy, the members of Zoar Mennonite and Hillsdale Bible Churches, the nurses at St. Mary's in Enid, our incredible family, and of course, my wife and son, Gret and Ricky. None of this would have been possible without a single one of you. We also realize the list would be endless if everyone who played some part of seeing us through was listed. For those, and you know who you are, we appreciate your willingness to support and love us during a rough time in our family's life.

Personally, I thank those of you who listened to me ramble on about what was happening in my life. Your patience allowed these thoughts to become a part of me.

To Cal, Drew, Don Moses, Gloria, Dorothy, thank you for reading over the manuscripts and giving me input in how to make it more readable. Also, thank you to Gret for the many times she looked it over for mistakes and for being patient with me while I spent time with my computer.

To Ricky, thanks for letting Daddy do "whatever it is he is doing" in his office. I have learned much from you, as well. You're one incredible man, and I know God has big plans for you. Stay faithful.

Last, but not the least, we need to thank our God above for being faithful to us and patient with us as we travel along life's pathways. He has seen us through many things that would have been impassible without His help. He is a great and awesome God and our prayers are that you can catch a large glimpse of Him in this book.

Table of Contents

Introduction

Ryan's Story

Chapter One...Does God have a "wonderful plan for our lives?"

Chapter Two...Does God hold grudges?

Chapter Three...Does God answer our prayers?

Chapter Four...Is God my co-pilot?

Chapter Five...God is great, God is good...?

Chapter Six...Is the church full of hypocrites?

Chapter Seven...How's the view from the cheap seats?

Chapter Eight...The B-I-B-L-E, is that the Book for me?

Chapter Nine...Does God <u>really</u> care about you?

Chapter Ten...What's the point of it all?

Afterthought

Notes

INTRODUCTION

On December 31, 1996, our life as a family took a horrible turn. This book is an attempt to explain that journey. Our intentions are not to take you down the same path, but meet you on yours and come out together.

Life is difficult. There are problems of every kind and every degree--we will all face some. How we react to the events on that journey is critical to survival. All along the path are the remains of those who did not make it. We almost became those remains, and possibly you are stuck, grasping for anything to get you going again. That is what this book is about--SURVIVAL! Spiritual survival, that is.

Where is God when we are stuck? What is He trying to teach us? Questions, questions, questions. We all have them. Are we going to answer every question you have? No. That is not our purpose. What you must realize is that as long as you are asking questions, you are okay. Maybe as you read our journey you can discover where you are in yours and pull yourself out of the trap you are currently in. Moving is critical--even when it is slow (barely moving is better than not at all.)

Our prayer for you is that through the words of this book you come out triumphantly in the end. How can you do that? We invite you to read on and see how our questions about God turned our tears into triumph.

Ryan's Story

December 31, 1996

After a month of intense study and concern about our unborn child's absence of growth and a small amniotic sac, Gretchen was admitted to the hospital to have the child the next day. Our excitement was building as we thought of having the first child of 1997 in the city where the hospital was located. Even though it was a couple of weeks early for him to be born, we were in good spirits. After all, our first son was one month early and everything turned out okay with him. That dream was soon interrupted by nurses entering the room like a den of ants, going here and there as though something was happening.

"What's going on?" we asked. They stated that the monitor attached to Gretchen's stomach had indicated a deceleration in the baby's heart rate, signaling that he was under stress and had to come out sooner than expected.

"How much sooner?" The nurses responded, "Right now!"

We were having a baby that night! We were shocked. What had happened? We were planning a quiet New Year's Eve in the hospital, but now it didn't look like that was going to be true. The doctor came in a little later to tell us what was going on, and to say that the baby was going to be small, but otherwise things were normal.

As the nurses prepared Gret for surgery, I went to a lounge on the second floor and waited until they came and got me. My mind was whirring. I wondered if everything was going to be okay, with the baby, and with my wife. After what seemed like an hour (but probably wasn't that long), a nurse arrived to direct me to where she was.

I found her strapped to a bed with doctors and nurses all around her. I barely recognized the shaking and frightened woman lying there. I made small talk with her, talking about things I'm sure she wondered about, or barely even cared about at that time. Nonetheless, there we were, in surgery, about to have our second child. An eternity passed as we waited for some kind of news.

At 6:14 p.m., the anesthesiologist told us that the baby was out and we had ourselves a boy. We waited impatiently for the healthy cry of a newborn child. There was nothing but silence until we heard a quiet mewing as if a small kitten was someplace in the room. It was our son. A few minutes later, the doctor came around the corner holding a bundle of blankets with a 4 pound, 5.8 ounce baby boy wrapped inside.

"Is he okay? Does he have all his fingers and toes?" The barrage of questions we all ask came out. "He's fine," the doctor responded.

Everything *was* fine as I rode the elevator back up to the nursery. In my arms was my second son, Ryan Anthony. Little did we know how things were changing already, but at that moment the joys of being a parent were rushing in and the tears were flowing.

"Everything's going to be alright," I thought as I looked into the face of that small child. The stress, the fear, the worry, was slowly fading into the past as I laid him onto the nursery bed. God had blessed us with what we thought was a healthy child, and we were thankful.

January 9, 1997

The numbness of joy related to having a new baby was quickly wearing off. There was obviously something wrong with our new baby, yet no clear cut diagnosis had been given. He had signs that indicated problems, possibly severe or life-threatening.

The ones I noticed were his malformed feet (called rocker bottom), and his tiny fingers crossing over one another (called overlapping digits). What did all this mean? Nothing to us. We just wanted to take our baby home, yet we couldn't because of the difficulty he was having with breathing and feeding.

Finally, after a week, the doctors told us what they thought he had, something called Trisomy 18. What's that? We didn't know. What did that mean for Ryan? Nobody would say. Those questions and a hundred others flooded our minds. We wanted everything we could get our hands on about this condition, yet the doctors were reluctant to give it to us because they weren't sure that was what he had. They didn't want to scare us without cause. Not knowing was killing us more than knowing, so we pursued it on our own. All we knew was that our baby's life could very well be taken from him, and our hearts broke as we held him, still connected to monitors and oxygen.

What we found wasn't good. We hoped Ryan didn't have it. What was it? Without going too deeply into the medical language (which I know nothing about), in each of us there are 23 pairs of chromosomes. With Trisomy 18, the 18th set has three rather than the normal two chromosomes. How this happens and why, I don't know. What did it mean for Ryan? Most likely, an early death, possibly 3-6 months.

Our world came crashing in on us. We immediately went before our God to petition Him for a miracle. Trisomy 18 was a killer, and we begged God to somehow make it so that Ryan didn't have it. The blood samples were taken and sent off to Oklahoma City. All we could do was wait for the results, not that easily, nor patiently, of course.

He had a possible fatal condition. We could do nothing but wait, and pray. We called upon our God to hear us and answer us. Above all, we saw our dependence upon Him, and we banked on Him to see us through.

January 9th-14th

Trisomy 18!!! How can this be happening? What did we do wrong? How could God do this to us? Now our lives were *really* crumbling before us and there was nothing we could do to stop it, except one thing: pray. We had to go before our God and beg for our son's life. And that is what we did. We were specific with Him, "God, in all Your strength and power, do not let our son have Trisomy 18. If he does, with a miracle, remove it. We don't care how it gets done, just do something." What were we doing? Praying for a miracle, nothing more, nothing less. Did we think a miracle would happen? A part of us didn't believe—that part that heard the doctors' burden of proof that made them think he had Trisomy 18. Another part knew that if God wanted to, He could. There was nothing and no one stopping Him. It was all a matter of whether that was God's plan or not.

We told our doctor how we had prayed for a miracle. Of course, he knew what God could do if He wanted, and it was his prayer too. We all wondered and waited as the tests were sent off to Oklahoma City.

The tests were complicated and required a multitude of circumstances that must be exactly right before they could be determined with any accuracy. One attempt was made at making the cells grow but failed. Another attempt was made. It also failed. In the meantime, there we were falling apart as we waited for those critical results and all we received was, "We can't get the cells at the precise time to get the results". This added to our frustration and our patience wore thin! We needed those results because they would determine everything that we had to decide concerning our son.

Finally, after 6 days and three attempts the results came back. I'll never forget the call that day. Gret and I were in the hospital room waiting for the results. The phone rang and Gret picked it up. Our doctor told her that they were successful in the test and they had determined that Ryan DID NOT have Trisomy 18!!! Her response? "You're kidding!" His reply? "You asked for a miracle didn't you?"

What did we feel? Complete release. Overwhelming emotions. Tears poured out as we held each other. As I read over my journal entry from that day, tears of joy are falling down my face. Here's a part of that entry: "Father, words do not nor could ever accurately describe my feelings nor my thanks to you. You have proven yourself to us again and we praise God! Ryan's tests are negative! NO TRISOMY 18."

February 7-12

Things were progressing well. Although Ryan was still not doing as well as we had hoped, plans were being made for us to take him home on Saturday the 8th. Gret was working hard at learning all the different things that were going to be needed for Ryan's stay. There were medicines, monitors, oxygen bottles, 'the wedge' (an incline he slept on to keep reflux to a minimum), tubes in his nose for feeding, methods of CPR for children, and on top of that, she had the normal baby stuff. Nurses were spending large amounts of time with her, doing all they could to help (something that meant the world to us). There was excitement in everyone. It had been over a month now since Ryan had been born. Everyone had grown attached to him and were rooting for him. The whole scene was incredible.

We were making plans at home. Baby beds were going up, things were being cleaned, and so on. Our older son, Ricky, was becoming excited. After having a little brother for a month, he was actually going to get to be near him, to hold him, etc. He was walking on air.

So were Gret and I. We were ready to get out of the hospital. It had been a long road, but we had made it. We were going home with our new son. We couldn't wait.

Wednesday, the 5th, I left for seminary, arriving with the good news that we were going to get to take Ryan home. I couldn't wait for that week to get over with. It was hard to concentrate on class items, but I struggled through them.

Finally, it was time to head home. I left around 7 a.m. on Friday, so that I could make it to the hospital by noon. All the way home I was thanking God for getting us through, and for the way He had provided for us and giving us the energy to do all the things. I also thanked Him for Gret, who had worked so hard for the son she loved. You could see it in the way she listened to the medical jargon of the nurses, the way she cared for Ryan, and the hundreds of other things she subjected herself to for this little baby.

Arriving at the hospital, I went upstairs to the maternity ward to look into the window of the nursery for Ryan. I was surprised and confused when I found the shades pulled. They were normally open, but today they weren't.

I softly knocked on the door for the nurses to let me in. As I entered, I asked, "Why are the shades pulled?" Their response caused fear and worry to flood through me. "There have been some changes in Ryan's condition, and we better let the doctor talk to you."

I walked over to the bed where Ryan was. When I had left him earlier in the week, things were okay. Now he was struggling and seemed to be barely hanging on. I couldn't understand how things could change so rapidly. How could he be ready for the trip home one day, and the next be on the verge of dying? There was obviously changes as I watched him. He was working just to breathe, his tiny chest collapsing every time he would take a breath. He looked so bad. I couldn't help but cry as I stood there in shock, staring at him.

When Gret arrived, we met with the doctor and was told that Ryan had had a rough night. His lungs were filling with fluid, he had had numerous events where his heart rate had dropped below 20 per minute, and had practically stopped breathing. One time they even had to bag him and give him CPR for almost two minutes before he responded. (I now knew why the shades were pulled.) We were told that it would be best if we stayed in the hospital that night because there was a strong possibility that he wouldn't make it until morning.

So, we stayed there, but didn't sleep the entire night. Most of it was spent in conversation about what we were to do, some of it was spent in prayer, and all of it was spent in tears as we contemplated the fact our baby was not going to live. We were afraid to fall asleep, mainly because we were certain that as soon as we did, the nurses would come wake us, informing us that Ryan had died. Hours went by and nothing happened.

At 6 a.m., a nurse came in and told us that Ryan had just had a major event where CPR was administered. We hurriedly got ready and went to the nursery. Inside was the doctor, a few nurses, and a hospital chaplain (not a good sign). As we stood around the bed, we discussed our options. It was finally stated that Ryan "was going to die anyway."

What did we feel? I told the chaplain that it would be best if we were left alone for a moment as we began to cry uncontrollably. We stood there for a moment or two, then went to our room to gather our thoughts.

It was out, Ryan was as good as dead. I didn't believe it though. This doctor was not our normal doctor (ours was out of town) and I needed to hear it from our doctor who was also a good friend of ours, one in whom we could trust. I chased him down by phone and discussed his associate's comments and what we were to do and think from here. We talked with the chaplain in our room. We called relatives and our former pastor and friend, trying to find someone to help us in this ordeal.

No one could do a thing for us. Even we were helpless

and now, maybe a little hopeless. Where had things fallen out of control? Where had God overlooked something? Had He lost control?

February 13-14th

It was obvious that Ryan wasn't going to survive. We were at our rope's end, and had no idea of where to go from there. We were grasping for anything to hold on to, but found little comfort. Deep down, we didn't know what to feel. Do we give up on Ryan? Or, do we keep going, doing everything we could for him? After many sleepless nights, and hours of prayer, and gallons of tears, we decided that we wanted to do some things differently.

First of all, were we prolonging what was inevitable by allowing the nurses to administer what was seen as heroics to revive our son? Were we being unfair to Ryan by going to such efforts just to say that "we kept him alive"? How could we tell if this was what God wanted us to do? These are just a few of the questions we had, and answers were difficult to come by (not that they could be answered).

We finally decided that we wanted to discontinue the "heroics" that were being administered, yet needed to do something for him to get the nourishment he needed. Eating was still very difficult for him, and it was a concern for us and the doctors. Even though we wanted the heroics to stop, insuring his God-given rights of food, air, etc. was a must. We had been made responsible for him by God and we couldn't just sit there and do nothing because of his trouble eating. That would be going too far.

As a result, we heeded our doctor's request that we travel to Oklahoma City to a specialist who could surgically install a feeding tube directly into Ryan's stomach. It would be better for him, and more convenient for us.

We arrived on Thursday afternoon and prepared Ryan for

his overnight stay before the surgery. Because of his DNR (Do not resuscitate) status, no monitors were attached to him for the first time since his birth. Deep down, we never thought he'd make it through the night, much less the surgery. He was very weak, and was having several episodes a day where he would practically die, but somehow would recover. Because of his tenacity for life, we were now in a strange surrounding, preparing for something we had no idea of how it would end.

The next morning, we got up early, ate a good breakfast, and went to the hospital, preparing to be there all day. Ryan was still there, just as we had left him. His surgery was scheduled for around noon, so we began the business of all that entailed. We talked with nurses and doctors, signed papers, said prayers, and slowly became more nervous as the time gradually came nearer.

Just before he was to go in for surgery, the anesthesiologist came out to talk with us. He couldn't understand why this little baby was on a DNR status. We tried to explain what he had been through, but it was still tough to understand why a life so young was not going to be resuscitated. Finally, he told us that it was a hospital policy that all DNR's be lifted during surgery, and that nothing would happen to Ryan. After all, he had a personal policy that "no one dies on my table." We told him that if God wanted Ryan to live or die, we nor he could change anything about it and if, by chance, he did die, there would be no hard feelings from us. Again, he reassured us everything would be fine.

The doctor then got up and wheeled Ryan's bed into the operating room as we sat there in the waiting room wondering about all that was going on. We made small talk, not that we really had anything to say, but that it took our minds off what was going on inside us.

About ten minutes later, the anesthesiologist came out with a very shaken look on his face and his hands trembling. We thought, "It happened, Ryan is dead." Instead, the doctor said that as soon as they attempted to put the IV in Ryan to put him under, he had essentially died, and they had administered CPR. He asked if we could talk somewhere, so we went to a private room where we met with him and the surgical doctor.

In the course of the conversation, they both informed us that if they were to perform this surgery, Ryan would probably never recover. In other words, he would be a vegetable. He would most likely be on a ventilator for life, however long that was. We knew we didn't want that. Their recommendation to us was that this "baby needed to go home to die. Don't let him die in a cold institution, but in a warm, loving home."

The anesthesiologist told us that we had been the most courageous parents he had ever seen. This was something that had never happened to him and it had shaken him. We were calm and seemed to have it all together. Little did he know how little we really "had it together." We told him that if it was not for a faithful God who had been with us, we would be falling apart, and at times had even thought about quitting. We couldn't do that because this was our son, and we had no choice but press on for his sake.

Within one hour we were heading back to Enid again. We were no farther than when we had left. The only difference now was that we had two more doctors' viewpoints that Ryan wasn't going to make it. In fact, it was almost certain that his life would be very short, and the day was near. But, still, no one had any diagnosis, other than he wasn't going to live long.

The month of February

The month was getting long. We could see that we were running out of resources physically, emotionally, and financially. What were we going to do? Where could we go to get help?

There seemed to be no one and nowhere to turn.

Gret had not been working for an extra month, something that we could not afford because of me being in seminary. Finances were running very low, as in, non-existent. Our storehouse was empty and we had no place to go for help. Or, so we thought.

That is when the family of God kicked into gear. God showed his love and concern in magnificent ways. He taught us a lesson in trusting Him.

First, the seminary, through donors, has a fund established to help students in extreme financial situations. As a result, we were awarded a gift of several hundred dollars equaling the amount Gret would receive for the month's salary.

Secondly, an area church took a special offering and presented close to $300.

Thirdly, an area restaurant had a special evening where 10% of earnings that night would be given to us, totaling close to $200.

Fourthly, our home church took up a special love offering for us one Sunday morning and presented us with over $1,500.

Fifthly, the church where I was interim pastor was faithfully praying for us, and giving us support where value can't be determined.

There were others, too many others, who gave of themselves through meals provided, food in our freezer, help around the house, and on and on. The family of God rallied around us and encouraged us beyond imagination. We had found our place to turn, and they were our brothers and sisters in whom we could trust.

As I type this and think back, I still am overwhelmed by God's provision through His body. We were down and people helped us in any way they could, even offering more than we could ever use.

Will we ever repay those people? I'd love to. Could we? In no way, shape, or form, would I pretend to think that we ever could. Do they expect us to? No. They gave of themselves and God will bless them. That is their reward, and our prayer.

The end of February and into March

It was inevitable. Big decisions had to be made. The medical world, as a whole, was not offering us much hope that Ryan would survive. Many of those who had worked closely with him had given him 3-6 months to live. What do we do now?

Should we take him home so that we could spend more time with him like the specialist had recommended? Or, should we leave him in the hospital where he was under constant medical care? If he does come home, how will we deal with all the "stuff" that comes along with him? Things were so overwhelming. At times, we thought there were no easy decisions to be made in life anymore. Everything was so complicated.

Finally, we decided to take him home so that if he was to die, we could be with him. This would give his older brother, Ricky, a chance to spend time with him, as well as, other family members. On February 24th, Ryan was out of a hospital for the first time. Fifty-four days in hospitals had come to an end. We were at home with our sons. Yet, things were not over.

Because of Ryan's condition, he was sent home with Hospice Care. There were tubes, monitors, oxygen bottles, feeding tubes and machines, medicines, and on and on. This was no normal "take your baby home and enjoy life" situation. Things were very complicated, something we were beginning to expect in life.

Either way, we *were* glad to be out of the hospital. We are thankful for those who serve others through Hospice. We could have never kept our sanity if it were not for the folks at that office and for the nurses who spent so much time with us. Without them, we couldn't have had Ryan at home at all because of the demands he placed on us. As a result, we were able to see our son in HIS crib, hold him, talk to him, and the many other things we wouldn't have had he stayed in the hospital.

Through it all, though, we began to wonder about God. Things seemed so hopeless. Days were filled with pressure. We couldn't make any sense out of the whole ordeal. Our perspective on things was not good. Was God's perception the same? We only wondered.

The month of March

Time had come to a halt. Things were at a standstill. In a sense, we didn't know what to expect next, so we just waited. We definitely didn't expect Ryan to live to the end of the month. Believe it or not, though, he was still there, plugging away.

In the middle of it all we wanted some answers from God. We knew that all we had to do was go to the Bible and He would provide all the answers to every question we had. After all, the Bible was "Life's Manual," we just needed to dive into it and find the mysteries of life.

We were given verses by friends that sometimes helped and made sense, but other times they seemed to hurt us more than help us (the verses, that is.) The part that bugged us most was that we knew these verses by heart, but they didn't bring the comfort we needed, nor did they answer ANY of the questions we had.

It was like we were being told, "Take two verses and call me in the morning." You know what, though? The next day, the heartache was still there as powerful as ever. The medication was not working and we were wondering about the "manual" and its true effectiveness.

The month progressed and things had not changed. Ryan was struggling. He was having moments where he would not breathe for several minutes, even when we did the "heroics" that worked before. He wasn't getting better, and we knew that any day he would be called home. Deep down, discouragement had crept in and we were giving up. As painful as it was, we were loosening our grip on Ryan and telling God that he was His and could do what He so desired. Honestly, we didn't know what else to do.

Early April

On April 7, I called the geneticist in Oklahoma City. We wanted some more information about what was going on with Ryan. They had talked like he wouldn't last a week or more once out of the hospital, but here it was a full month later. We wanted to know some details on how sure they were of the diagnosis given to him, how they had come to that conclusion, and the chances of them being wrong.

The phone call was long and I'm sure she could sense the frustration in my voice as I asked question after question. It probably sounded like I was attacking her credibility, which I wasn't. Instead, the medical field was not impressing us with their forecasts. There was a lot to be desired in the whole ordeal.

After close to an hour, the doctor informed me that if she had made an incorrect diagnosis, Ryan could very well live up to 4 to 5 years of age. He would need loads of attention, would never function "normally," and could very well be bed-ridden for that entire time. She, in essence, was saying that Ryan would be a "vegetable."

The news hit hard. There were changes to be made. A new plan of attack was needed. Should we be more aggressive with occupational therapy, physical therapy, etc. and move out of the hospice mode? Or should we look into a home for him? What did this mean for the seminary career I was in the middle of? One of us would need to be around the house to care for him, so some major life changes were coming.

Once again, things were crashing in on us, and more big decisions had to be made. In the midst of it all, we wondered, "Is God concerned that we are about to go under water? Has He possibly abandoned us? What happened to the promise, 'I will never leave you nor forsake you'"?

Deep down, we began to think that God wasn't concerned for us anymore, and that hurt us deeply because He had been the bedrock in which our anchor had been attached to our entire lives. Without His care and concern, how could we go on? We couldn't, that was the problem!

April 9-11, 1997

Preparing to return to Dallas for classes, we went to bed "early". Things had been progressing as normal. We were tired, confused, and wondering how God would work in all this. We had been making so many big decisions the past few months that our heads hurt. Stress was high, emotions charged, and hearts aching. We were doing what we could to trust God to do what was best. Some days that was easier than others.

Things changed at 2:30 a.m., April 9th. We were awakened by Ryan crying, or at least making more noise than normal. Since I was needing the sleep for the busy day ahead, Gret got up and went into the living room with him.

He continued making noise, and I finally joined them. We thought maybe we should give him the medicine prescribed to help him rest and relax in such situations. So, we walked in the dark toward the kitchen with Ryan still making noise.

As we turned on the light he did two very strange things we have yet to understand today. One, he immediately got quiet. Completely peaceful. Secondly, he struggled to focus on the light. That may not seem too odd, but for Ryan, who had yet to gaze at things, it was. Not only that, he was craning his neck to the left to do so, which was odd because his natural turn had been to the right. In fact, in past weeks, we had been working with him in helping to move his neck the other way. Tonight, he needed no help.

As he did so, I was preparing the proper does of medicine. Gret called it to my attention by saying, "Leland, look at him." We both stopped for a moment to enjoy this new step for him, then I went back to the task of medicine.

Once the medicine was over, I took him into my arms, walked back into the living room, plopped down onto the couch, and began to pat him on the bottom. Gret followed and turned off the light as she walked by. Immediately he began to cry again. I started to rock a little and sing to him hoping that he would calm down, which he did after about 5 minutes.

At about 2:55 I noticed that I thought he was having another spell of not breathing. It was hard to tell because there were times that he was breathing, but it was so shallow you couldn't tell. I quietly mentioned to Gret that I didn't think he was breathing. We both looked at the clock.

Time went by in slow motion as it always had when he was doing this. I still hadn't felt anything. Then, he took a deep breath and exhaled. I looked at the clock--3:01 a.m. More time passed and nothing happened. Finally, at about 3:15 I told Gret that I thought he was either not breathing, or was fast asleep. "At 3:20 let's check," I said.

The time came, Gret turned on the nearby kitchen light, and I laid Ryan forward gently to not wake him up.

We immediately knew he had left us. We just sat there for a moment looking at him. He looked so beautiful, so peaceful, so calm, so precious. He had gone without a fight, no screaming out in terror, nothing. He had just passed on to the other side.

We then realized that we needed to call Hospice to let

them know that we thought Ryan had died. So, we laid him on the floor as I dialed the phone number.

We then called my family who all lived within a block of our house. With family around us, our hospice nurse, came in and began going about the business of preparing him for what was ahead. Within a few minutes, the funeral home men showed up and began their task of preparing *us* for the funeral arrangements.

Finally, around 6 a.m., everyone was gone, including Ryan. We were left alone to begin thinking of how we were going to break the news to Ricky, a task that neither of us was ready for. At around 7, we went into his room and woke him up.

After a few minutes of small talk, and allowing him to gather his thoughts, we began the "speech." After being told that Ryan had died last night, he hung his head and responded, "I guess I'm not a big brother anymore." We all three began to cry. My heart was breaking inside (and still is as I type). He had been an awesome brother, caring for and loving a little brother who would not grow up and be his buddy. He had been a trooper through it all, and had taught me so much about faith, trust, prayer, and God.

I told him that he would always be a brother, only his brother lived in Heaven. That seemed to lift his spirit. We then explained what was ahead for us as a family. There would be funeral home visits, people over, phone calls, culminating in a funeral.

The next two days were a whirlwind. Events took place so fast. We chose a casket. We called a friend who would oversee the funeral. We picked the clothes Ryan would wear. We picked Friday at 4 for the funeral. And, we cried a lot. We struggled to remain positive. With our emotional stability already drained, we could feel ourselves wearing thin. Only through God's strength could we make it.

Friday finally came. We had chosen to not have an open

casket at the funeral because of the potential for so many small children, especially the many Gret had spent time with as an elementary teacher. We didn't want them to be distracted by the thoughts of little Ryan being dead, and miss what our friend was going to be saying up front (who was preparing a message targeted for them).

The day was extremely cold and windy, just like our lives had been the past few months. The service was powerful. Barry gave a tremendous message and God got us through the day. At last, we went home to a house where Ryan would never be again. A chapter in our lives had closed. What would the future hold? We didn't care as the three of us collapsed on the bed together.

Though Ryan's story ends here, ours doesn't. In the next few pages we want to take you through some of the life lessons we encountered as we watched our son progress through life and into eternity.

We pray you can glean ideas from them that will help you in your journey. More importantly, we hope you'll be able to see things from a different perspective than maybe you have before. As we talk about the book, let me quote a friend, "It doesn't solve any of the problems . . . it simply provides a new set of lenses to look through for the grieving family, a family hit by tragedy . . . and a real life situation to use as a back drop to work through some of the greatest problems still out there!"

chapter

Does God have a "wonderful plan" for our lives?

I am always fascinated by the stories in the Bible that hint at (without coming out and saying it) God's divine plan. My favorites are in Ruth 2:3 and 4:1. I love the way the author puts it, "...and *she happened to come* to the portion of the field belonging to Boaz..." and, "...*and behold*, the close relative of whom Boaz spoke was passing by,..." (italics mine).

If Ruth had not 'happened to come' to that field, her whole story would be meaningless. But, because she 'happened to come' to that field, she was used by God to be the matriarch of the incredible King David (4:16-22). Did she happen to do anything? Was it purely coincidence that she stopped in Boaz's field? I don't think so. There was much more to the story than mere coincidence, and the author hints at that. God had directed her. Nothing more, nothing less.

In the second example, Boaz is organizing the process needed to purchase the land of Naomi's family (which would also give him access to what he really wanted, the hand of Ruth in marriage.) He wanted that right, but according to 3:12 found himself second in line. Following the custom, he went to the city gates where the business always took place. He would need two things to occur before he could purchase the land: 1) The person with the first shot at buying the land (the closest relative) needed to be there, and, 2) that person must not want the land. Arriving at the gates, Boaz surely found the elders there. The only thing lacking was that closest relative. But, BEHOLD, guess who comes along, "the very man Boaz had been talking about." (The old saying, "Speak of the devil" comes to my mind). In verses 2-10, we see the events that follow, resulting in Boaz acquiring the land in question, the hand of Ruth in marriage, and the city's leaders' blessings. All of these events just 'happened' to occur because "BEHOLD, the very man" showed up. Once again, purely coincidence? Definitely not. God had directed and orchestrated each and every detail of that day so that those events could and would take place.

God does have a plan for us. Everything in a day follows that plan. Things are not accidents, even when they seem to be out of control. Circumstances just don't 'happen' to happen, they are orchestrated by God to come about. This bothers some people because of the bad events that take place. They cannot handle the fact that God knows about "bad" events before they happen, yet does nothing about them. Those feelings are well understood. I want to challenge those people that feel this way to look at it from a different angle, though.

Let's begin with the positive. When good things take place in life we immediately give God the credit, calling them blessings. "He has been so good to us. He has provided. Isn't He wonderful?" And so on. God's plan is marvelous, beyond our wildest dreams. In fact, during those times we are glad God is on our side, and His plan is absolutely perfect. We are comforted by the knowledge that God's plan is working out to our benefit, and we like the thought of our lives fitting into that plan.

Then troubles come. All of a sudden, God's plan isn't good enough anymore. We want Him to fix the wrong. When He doesn't do it immediately and exactly as we wanted, we start to throw verbal insults at Him. We doubt Him. We doubt His goodness. We question His love—that all-encompassing love that is supposed to heal everything. The plan that once comforted us brings anger and resentment to the surface. We no longer want to be a part of that plan.

How could God do this to me? Why me? What is He doing? Notice, all of these questions have nothing to do with God's plan, but rather have everything to do with His character. It is not the plan we want to jump all over, it is God Himself. The issue is not with the plan, but with God. We want some of God, and we want Him NOW, and we expect Him to show up to explain His plan to us. Does He? Not always, sometimes, never.

We were in that position for over three months. We wanted to know God's plan, what He was doing, why us, and so on. His plan confused us because it was not "wonderful", in fact it was *no good!*

How can we be satisfied with God's good plan, but resent it when things don't go as we would want them? Why do the bad events cast a disparagement upon God? Has He suddenly lost control? Has His plan somehow gone awry?

My proposition is this. When tough times come, and they will, rather than begin doubting God's plan, look hard at yourself. Those times may say more about yourself than they do about God and His plan. What do I mean? Personally, during Ryan's life, the way I reacted to bad events and bad days said nothing about God, but everything about me. Did I really believe God's plan had been altered? Did I really believe God's plan was letting me down? Even though I didn't know God's plan, was I comfortable with Him being in control? That's it! I wanted to be in control of that "plan", and I wasn't. Right there is my problem. It isn't that *God* is in control that bothers me, it's that I *am not*. If I can just work through that, those difficult times take on a new meaning.

God is in control. He has a plan that brings the best possible results for me, not always being filled with good things and easy days along the way. Can I deal with that? Can I surrender to that plan, and be content (not necessarily comfortable) with it?

Those who can't do the above, usually find themselves in a decaying relationship with God. If it all can't be reconciled in their mind, they end up doubting God to the extent that He is rejected.

What does all this have to do with our family? Ryan's birth, life, and death, the whole sequence of events, was perfect timing and though the situation was not pleasant, we knew that there was a plan. Don't get us wrong, we did not and still do not *like* the plan, but are convinced that there is more to the plan than what we are seeing on this level. How can we say that Ryan's life and death were perfect timing and as a result drew us to God rather than drove us away from Him? (The intent of the following examples is not to bore you, but to show those things which were God's confirmations along the way that kept us going.)

1. In the Spring of 1996 I had become a full-time student at Dallas Theological Seminary, commuting five hours to Dallas each week. One of the requirements for all students with 9 or more hours is health insurance, something we didn't have nor could afford. I really resented the fact that where we had been operating on faith in God to protect us, we were now forced to place that faith in an insurance company. After a few attempts to be excused, I finally "gave-in" and purchased insurance. If we had not had that insurance, our family's finances (already stretched) would have been completely devastated. Remember Ruth's "just so happened"? It just so happened that we HAD to purchase health insurance, something that without Dallas Seminary's prompting we would have never had. Perfect timing.

2. My wife and I "planned" the prospective date of arrival of Ryan by counting the months and days, then calculating when

he would be born (Jan 17, 1997). With all the complications of the final month of pregnancy, we were worried that I'd be back in Dallas when he would be born, rather than be by Gret's side. Instead, he "just so happened" to be born while I was at home for Christmas break. Not only that, he was born early enough I could spend time with him. Time that ended up being in the hospital, talking with doctors about the future, and dealing with the situation. Had he been born according to our schedule, I *would have* been in Dallas. Once again, perfect timing.

3. Once we realized there were problems, we had to decide if I was going back to school for the semester, or should sit out. After hours of prayer, discussions with the doctor, and calls to friends, we decided I should keep going.

Our pediatrician felt that we weren't looking at any *serious* problems, so it would be best to continue. Of course, as time went by we began to doubt that advice because things were not going so well. In retrospect, though, we believe that seminary was part of God's plan in helping us deal with the whole ordeal. The doctor's comments 'just happened' to keep us going.

Because I continued seminary, it gave me opportunity to know more closely professors I would not have otherwise known; gave me access to several people that encouraged us along the way; and gave us hundreds, if not thousands, of people to pray for us. One other thing it supplied was the opportunity to write this book. Again, coincidence? No. Perfect planning and timing? Yes.

This list could go on, but we think we have made our point. God knows what He is doing, even when we may not. His plan, though not guaranteed easy, and as stated earlier, not necessarily liked, is good. Do we still wonder what it was all about? Do we still question His plan? Yes, to both of these. But, we have also decided that we would rather be a part of His plan (good or bad), than not be a part of that plan.

It must be realized, God is sovereign, and though His plan may not fit ours, His is best to follow. Even when we are completely confused by His plan and seem very lost, it's critical to be content with His actions, and to trust in Him completely that He knows what He is doing and that He cares for us.

All that has been said is not an easy item. It's a tough concept to grasp, not just for those new or weak in faith, but, also for those that have been around the block a time or two. We hope the reader understands that we are not saying we have it all together or that it is an easy '1-2-3' process. Instead, we are saying that it can be done, but will take a mental awareness and commitment to not allow yourself to go down the road of doubt too far before turning around and returning to the road of faith.

Back to the question, "Does God have a "wonderful plan for our lives"? We still honestly believe the answer is yes, even after the fact that we have buried our son, to be sure, *not* a wonderful thing! How can we say this then?

When someone says that God has a wonderful plan for your life, it should not imply that everything in this life is going to be wonderful. In fact, if anyone guarantees you that your life will be wonderful after trusting Christ, they are lying to you. Life just begins at salvation, and difficult times will come, expect them. How can being saved be so wonderful then? God does have a plan, and it is good, to the fullest degree. But, that doesn't mean that this life will be *all* good. The ultimate will come when we stand in the presence of God and will be accepted as one of His own (Rom. 5:1). *That* is the wonderful plan He has for our lives. *That* is what makes THIS life all worthwhile. *That* is what gives us hope to stick it out when we'd much rather quit. *That* is what we have to grab hold of, and hold tightly to, when the winds of life blow against us. *That* is what will keep us from doubting God and ending up by the wayside in a heap of ruins (remember the remains mentioned in our introduction?).

God is good, and doubting that goodness is exactly what Eve did when the serpent tempted her with the fruit of the forbidden tree. We must be bigger than that, and refuse to allow him the satisfaction of knowing that he caused another child of God to fall away. God is good, and His plan is best and we know that He loves and cares for us...beyond what we can see in this difficult situation. That is the fuel for our faith to keep us pressing on, when we'd much rather press STOP!

(A side note I'd like to add here...in the middle of a situation, it is healthy to step back and "count your blessings" similar to what I did with the listing of things earlier. No, it doesn't negate the negatives, but it does give you opportunity to look for the things that God may be doing in your life right now. Focusing on *whatever* positives you can find will do you much more good than sitting around re-thinking every negative. Just try it.)

chapter 2

Does God hold grudges?

What did we think? What did we feel? Shock. Disbelief. Fear. Confusion. Then someone asked us if we had started to blame one another for all that was taking place. That was a new and foreign thought—BLAME. Of course, we hadn't, and wouldn't. What we did do though was each of us began to blame ourselves.

First, Gret. After all, she had carried the child. Had she eaten something wrong? Had she done something in the first trimester to cause this? Had she laid wrong at night? What was it that did this? When I heard her ask these questions my heart broke. I knew it couldn't be her. She was the best mother I'd ever seen, loving and caring for the unborn child like no one else I knew. She was committed to taking vitamins, eating right, everything needed for a successful pregnancy. What could that mean? One thing, it must be *my* fault.

So, I took the ball and ran with it. What could I have to do with this problem? After hours of thinking of what I could've done, I figured it out. It must be God punishing me for my sins. Those hidden secrets were finally coming back to haunt me. All those times of rebelling against God had caught up with me, and now my son was paying my bills.

I was devastated. It had to be me, a process of elimination

had proven it. It wasn't Gret so it had to be me. It was that simple. Guilt overwhelmed me. Actually, it floored me. I couldn't shake it for at least two weeks. My Christian life was ruined. How could I come to God and ask for Ryan's healing when I was the cause?

I knew what I had done to cause this. In college I had made some horrible mistakes, and as a result had been involved in many things I knew were not pleasing to God. The most prominent that kept popping into my mind was the alcohol and drug abuse. I had become so dependent on those things to help me through my problems that it was a regular practice. For close to two years I had used alcohol nearly every day, and some type of drug nearly as often. What I had tried to cover up with good behavior was peeking its nasty head out and was taking the form of an unhealthy child.

Finally, one morning during my quiet time I broke down and pleaded with God, "Father, if something I have done has caused all this, I beg You to take it out on me. You can beat me up, bloody me, throw me in a ditch, and drive off, never to come back, but please, leave my son alone. He doesn't deserve it, I do. Come and get me." I prayed this prayer while crying uncontrollably, something I had not done in a long time. I wanted so badly to fix Ryan, especially if I was the cause.

All of a sudden I had this strange feeling come over me. No, it wasn't an angel sent from God, nor a loud audible voice, or even a burning bush in the backyard. It was just an overwhelming sensation that God was saying to me, "Leland, who do you think I am? What kind of God do you think I am? Who do you think you're serving? You came to the cross and trusted Christ to cover your sins, didn't you? Do you think that I wouldn't keep my end of the bargain? Your sins, past, present, and future, were covered on the cross, and have absolutely nothing to do with this situation."

What was all this? Nothing but God's grace rushing in on me and blowing me away. Sure, I knew about God's grace, but had never applied it to my life as God had. He had forgiven my sins, but I hadn't. I was still carrying them around with me like some kind of ball and chain. No wonder I had never experienced true joy in my life with Christ. I wasn't living the new life God had given me years before when I came to Him as my Savior.

This was a new thought. I didn't say anything to anyone because I was not sure I completely grasped everything I was thinking yet. I needed time to analyze, synthesize, and organize my thoughts. Could it be true that I did not need to *work* so hard to make God glad He saved me? Was there really forgiveness for sins to the point that I could live a life without my previous sins hovering above me like some kind of dark cloud? Does God hold a grudge, or does He really pour out grace like the Bible says?

Within a couple of weeks I returned to Dallas for classes, still wrestling with this issue. I wanted to believe the "voice" I had heard that morning, but it just seemed too good to be true. Complete forgiveness, what a thought. God's grace covering all my sins and allowing me to live when I deserved to die. Could God do that?

I found the answer during one of the lectures at seminary in Genesis two and three. In 2:16, God is very clear to Adam and Eve that He does not want them to eat the fruit of a certain tree. If and when they do, the punishment is laid before them...death. I don't believe Adam and Eve interpreted God to mean merely some kind of spiritual death (though that did occur). I believe they understood Him to mean that in the day they ate of the tree, they would surely DIE, as in kaput, zap, the end. What happens?

In chapter three, we see the serpent debating with Eve what God really said, or meant. After a short discussion, she sees that the fruit is good, in many ways. It not only will be delicious, it will make them like God (something they already were, see

1:27). After both ate, they realized they were naked and were ashamed, so they hid.

God comes for his daily walk, and cannot find the two, so He calls out for them. From the midst of the bushes they reply, "We heard you, but were afraid because we were naked." There goes the perfect environment, the perfect one-on-one relationship with God, the perfect transparent relationship with one another. Because they ate of the fruit God was now going to remove them, not just from the garden, but from the face of the earth altogether. After all, had He not said, "You shall surely die"?

What happens? God turns to the serpent (he must have been hiding in the bushes sneaking a peak at what was happening) and CURSES him.

Then, He turns to the woman. If it would have been me, my heart would have sank. His commandment and judgement for disobeying would have been ringing in my ears, especially the "shall surely die" part. Instead, God lets her know that in childbirth there will be pain, and all the days of her life will be lived in desire for her husband. Not exactly what she planned on hearing. I can see her, with this puzzled look on her face, not completely understanding what had just happened. Instead of being zapped, she was told that there was a future, and she was in it. How could this be?

Finally, to the man He turns and says, "Because of what you have done, I must put you both to death, because that is what I said I would do when you ate of the tree." No, not exactly. Instead, He CURSES the ground and lets Adam know that because of the curse, he will have to labor to get food (where once he had had a 24-hour buffet line). Adam, too, had a future. How could this be?

Why didn't God put the two out of their misery as He had said he would do? How could He let them live when He had said "you shall surely die"? The only explanation I can find is, GRACE and MERCY. Were there consequences for their actions? You bet there were. Were Adam and Eve disappointed in what they had done? You better believe it, and I'm sure they were reminded everyday about it. But, they were alive. Something neither was expecting to be after what they had done. Were they aware of God's grace and mercy? Most likely, and with every breath they took.

Does God hold grudges? I ask that question again. To the person who has come to the cross of Jesus and claimed its cleansing grace, there is complete forgiveness. The past, present, and future sins are gone, as in G-O-N-E (see Psalm 103, especially verses 9 and 12). Your filthy sins are washed and the stain is gone.

Are there consequences for sin? Remember Adam and Eve? They are proof that sin costs, sometimes dearly, but the fact that God still converses with them proves that He forgives and forgets those who truly repent. Isn't that amazing? Amazing grace? For us, that grace gave the reason to press on when we, at times, felt like pressing stop.

Now, I cannot continue without making a comment about something I brought up. Why did this happen if it wasn't a consequence for some sin I had committed? Does Ryan's illness have to be the result of sin? Let's look at a story in Scripture that may help us answer that.

Read the whole ninth chapter of John, then come back. That's right, put the book down, find a Bible, read it, then come back.

Did you read it? Then, let's go on with the story.

Jesus, while walking down the road one day comes across a man who had been blind since birth. The question is asked, "Who sinned, this man or his parents that he was born blind?"

Excuse me? Did I miss something here? Wasn't the man *born* blind? Then, tell me, how could he have sinned before he was born to cause this?

Yes, it is a dumb question. But, where did it come from? I'll tell you...bad theology. They obviously believed in a theology that said: 1) if good things are happening to you, then you must be living right, and, 2) if bad things are happening to you, then you must have messed up somewhere. This theology is not new on the scene of Jesus' day (see Job's friends' comments), nor is it uncommon today.

Now, before you say anything, let me confess. Yes, I had bought into that. How else could I assume that just because Ryan was sick meant someone was to blame? This bad theology just about ruined me. Please, be careful. Just because you live an "incredibly righteous" life does not guarantee blessing. Does it help? Yes. It can't hurt, but it definitely does not mean bad things won't happen to you. After all, remember where you are living—in a fallen, sin corrupted world that WILL guarantee heartaches and broken dreams. Also, just because bad things happen, it does not necessarily mean sin is involved, though it could.

Look at the story again, notice who asked the question. Not the blind man, but someone who felt that he wasn't as bad as another. That is how it usually works. Someone has a tragedy occur and everyone else starts coming up with the reason for it while the inflicted is left sitting by the gates without a clue of what is going on. Everyone else has his problem figured out but him. Please, for the sake of the person who is hurting, don't immediately start pointing fingers and leaving him sit in the darkness. Instead, help the person up. Together make things as bearable as possible.

Now, back to the text. Why was this man born blind? Not because of sin at all. Rather, he was born blind "...in order that the works of God might be displayed in him..." (translation: that God might be glorified). In other words, this man was a tool by which God's greatness was going to be displayed. His life of blindness had a reason, and it was not to show what sin could do, but what God could do. What an honor. What a privilege.

Fast forward to where you are today. Could God be using a horrible situation "in order that the works of God might be displayed" through you? Are you willing to sit by the gates of the city waiting for Christ to walk by and powerfully and wonderfully use you to glorify the Father? Tough question, huh?

Finally, back to the text one more time. I could not help but notice how God used this event. This story took one whole chapter to describe. The man in the story had to tell God's work time and time again to a hundred different people. He finally grew tired of it all and put a finger in the chest of the religious leaders and said, "You guys don't get it, do you? You can debate all you want about where Christ is from and how He did what He did. I can say this, I was blind, but now I see. I believe He is from God, and that settles it for me."

A few verses later Christ comes to the man, this time healing him of more than physical blindness. The man gains earthly sight and heavenly sight! What a story! God was truly glorified through it all. The man starts the chapter a poor, blind man and ends it becoming a rich, eternally seeing man. Praise the Lord.

To sum it all up, don't forget, God's grace is incredible. God does not hold grudges. The cross of Christ covered all sin, and forgiveness is available to anyone who comes to Him in repentance. Grace covers it all, no matter what you've done. Though guilty, guilty, guilty, we are justified (declared not guilty) by the grace of God. If you're struggling, go to Him and receive that free (and freeing) grace. Then, know that He is God and begin life as one who's no longer blind, but for His glory and through His power live as one who truly knows what life really is. Are you thinking about pressing stop? Do you want the energy to press on? That's it right there. Live like you know you can—forgiven and for the glory of the God Who saved you.

chapter 3

Does God answer our prayers?

Does God answer our prayers? Or sometimes, we wonder, does God even hear our prayers? If He does, why are they sometimes not the way we want them? If He doesn't, why do we waste the time in offering them? When we do pray, can we really change things through them?

When it comes to prayer, there are probably more questions than answers. It is such a difficult subject because all we have to go on is our perceived perspective of the situation. For instance, I pray for "x", then wait for God's response. After a while, I get "x". Other times, though, I get something like "zz". The answer is in no way close to what I prayed and I am left wondering what in the world went wrong. Maybe where I went wrong was when I selfishly prayed for only "x", instead of allowing God to use the whole alphabet.

With that, the question goes back to, "Does God hear our prayers?" In answering that, I want to ask another question, "What would it mean if God did *not* hear our prayers?" It would mean that 1) God is deaf, which is a ridiculous statement. 2) He does not get involved in the mundane affairs of our lives. We're left on our own to fend for ourselves. Which could be, but isn't true because of how the Bible makes it clear that God is involved in every detail of every person's life. (Ps. 139 is one example. If

He goes to such great trouble in designing me in the womb, why would He not care about the details of life? Also, He says "Ask anything in My name..." That doesn't sound like a non-caring statement). 3) He cares about our affairs, but He's unable to do anything about them. This one has many implications, all bad. Think through that one and see how many you can come up with. I'll give you one to get started. If He can't do anything about our prayer requests, how and why on earth would He deserve our worship as *God*? He isn't God if He isn't all-powerful. And He isn't all-powerful if He can't fix my tiny little problem. And why should I even pray if He can't do anything about them? Take it from there.

God does hear our prayers and *can* do something about them and does. Then why do so many needs/requests seem to go unanswered? To put it bluntly, I don't know. I am not God nor can I think like God. I don't know His plan for our lives and why sometimes our solutions cannot be used. The best I can do is use this illustration, but understand, it's limited.

My son and I were at a garage sale the other day. He found himself a nice looking used bicycle for $3. He came to me and asked me to buy it for him. I had to deny his request. He was mad at me for days, constantly reminding me about the bike I passed up for *three bucks*. Why? Because I don't care for him? No. Because I don't care to get involved in his mundane affairs? No. Well, it has to be because I care, but couldn't do anything about it. No, again. I had the three bucks in my pocket. "Then why on earth did you not buy your son the bike?" you shout. Because, coming up was his birthday, and in storage was a brand new, awesome bike that he had seen at a local store. I knew that something much better was in store, and if I granted his request for the $3 bike, the $60 one would not be needed. I wanted him to have the best, what he really *needed*, not just adequate, and what he *wanted*.

What does this illustration mean? Could it be that you've been asking for a $3 bike, and God has a new, shiny one waiting for you in the garage? God wants what is best, but can you wait for your birthday? Are you going to be mad at him for months because He wouldn't give you what you WANTED because He was sending what you NEEDED?

Sometimes I believe that is what happens. We get so caught up in what we want, that we refuse to see the situation from God's perspective.

"Yeah, but you don't understand the situation I am in and what I am praying for. This is big and God must answer me," you say. "You sound like you are defending God." You are right, it does sound that way, but I am defending God from a similar circumstance you are in. I was praying for my son's life, something I felt (and you probably agree) was big and God must hear. True, the situation may be different, but the principle is not. My requests were limited totally to my perspective, never looking for God's. I wanted what I wanted, and that was all.

In the course of things, we get impatient and angry and start throwing insults we really don't mean at God over something that is coming in its due time.

Does this solve everything? No, and I realize that. Hopefully, it does bring prayer into perspective though. Praying is not always getting, (getting what we want, that is.) "Very much of our modern prayer is vain because men approach God imagining that they have some claim upon God whereby He is under obligations to answer their prayers."[1] Just because we pray it, it doesn't obligate God to answer it. When it isn't answered, it doesn't necessarily say anything about God, but more about us.

God did answer our prayers about the Trisomy 18. Ryan didn't have it, which meant the world to us at the time. In fact, to this day we still believe it was a miracle that he didn't. Did God answer every prayer we had concerning Ryan? No, definitely not. In fact, there may be more "unanswered" prayers than answered ones with him.

You still are asking about prayer though and why do we do it if God already has the plan fixed? Good question. Let me restate it to match the opening of the chapter, Can I change things by praying? I think people tend to take it to extremes.

For those who believe God has the plan already etched in stone, prayer is pointless. It will all take place whether they pray for it or not, so they don't pray at all. They have taken it to extremes, and forgotten many key passages about prayer. On the other hand, there are those who believe that everything God does depends upon man. They think that God cannot and does not act without man's permission through prayer. They, too, have taken it to an extreme and forgotten many key passages about prayer. Which of the two are right? Both, and neither.

God does have a plan that's being played out before our very eyes that is unaffected by man's attempt to stop or change it. There are those things that may have happened completely different if man wouldn't have requested them from God. It isn't an issue of all or nothing, though. In other words, if God has that plan, it doesn't mean I don't pray for something to change. Also, just as wrong is that He has to wait on me and can't do anything unless told to do it. There must be a balance.

This gets tough, because how do we know what things can be changed through prayer and those that can't? How do I know what God is willing to do and how to pray in that circumstance? Again, here's the best my simple mind can do.

I, Ricky's father, have an incredible vacation planned this summer where we are going to an area lake and will fish for three days one holiday weekend. I have every last detail drawn up in my mind, down to how many fish we'll catch.

Ricky comes to me a couple of weeks before the trip with

a brochure of a lake a little farther away, but where the fishing is much more exciting. He doesn't know the details of the trip I have planned other than where it is and how long we will be gone.

He finally asks, "Dad, I have a request. Could we postpone the trip one week so we can go here (pointing to the brochure)? The fishing is much better, and the lake is prettier. I know it will take 5 days instead of three because of the travel time involved, but it will be worth it. Plus, if we wait, the lake won't be as busy for the holiday. What do you think?"

So, I think about it. I realize he's right. The lake won't be as busy, it is much prettier there, and most importantly, the fishing is far better. That settles it. We are going where Ricky has suggested.

Did Ricky know I would change my mind about this BIG trip I had planned until he asked me? No. Was he wrong for asking me for something different than I had planned? No. Am I glad he asked me about it? Yes, because of all the fish and fun we had. Why did he ask? Because he knew his father well enough to know that he could ask. That is critical. Why should we ask God for anything? Because we know our Father enough to know that we can ask Him anything and He does the best thing. Don't miss that, the key is the goodness of the Father, and that He'll do the best thing.

Ricky's request didn't change my purpose (fishing and fun), just my actions (what lake we went to). Again, realize this story can only take you so far in relation to how God actually works, but I think it helps get the point across.

Where on earth am I taking *you*? Let's look at two biblical accounts that may help answer that question.

Exodus 32:9-14. Let's get the context. Moses is up on Mt. Sinai with God, receiving the 10 commandments. The nation of Israel is at the bottom thinking Moses has died because he had been gone so long. They commence in building a golden calf and proclaim that this is their God who brought them out of Egypt. God notices their ignorance and becomes provoked (a good way of saying, "He was MAD!"). At the end of verse ten he tells Moses to turn his head because He is about to annihilate the people at the bottom of the hill and it may be a little messy.

Moses steps up to the plate and takes a swing. "O LORD, how can you say you will destroy your chosen people? The nations around will say all kinds of bad things about you if you do that. Please, don't kill them. Change your mind about what you said you were going to do."

What is God's response? Look at verse 14: "So the LORD changed His mind about the harm which He said He would do to His people."

Let me ask you, did Moses' prayer change anything? Would God's move have been any different if Moses would have not prayed? Verse fourteen may have read differently had he not. We can only speculate.

Prayer does change things, but do we always get our exact request? Let's look at another example from scripture.

This one is in Matthew 26:39 and 42. Jesus is in the garden, deeply grieved about what is to take place in just a few hours. He drops to the ground before His Father in Heaven and prays, "If it is possible, let this cup pass from Me; yet not as I will, but as You will. . . if this cannot pass away unless I drink it, Your will be done."

What is His request? Plainly put, that the cross be removed from His future and another way to atone for the sin of mankind be utilized. Does He get His request? No. Why not? Christ's request was that if there was any other way to do what had to be done, let's find it. He was not praying for a change of purpose for God (sin's atonement), but a change of action (the cross and His awesome suffering) be determined. Was this possible? Obviously not, because if any person's prayer should have and could have been answered it would have been God's own Son.

From these two stories (and there are others) we learn that prayer does affect circumstances (Moses), but they do not HAVE to change them (Jesus).

How do we know what God will do unless we ask Him? How do we know that He will not do it unless we ask Him? If He chooses not to grant it, what should that mean to us and how should we respond? Unanswered prayers say more about us than they do about God. The way I react to God's "unwillingness" to answer my exact prayer says volumes about me (and my lack of faith), but very little about God. How can I say that? Let me explain.

You can see my reaction, hear my disappointed speech, etc., but God and His ultimate plan is not revealed that way. We don't know what He is doing in the situation, and there are times when He does not seem to be moving at all, but in reality He is moving mightily for us. Only time will tell, something we never give Him when it is our request being awaited.

Something to consider, too, is that sometimes what seems like an "unanswered" prayer is really an answered one. For instance, we prayed that Ryan would have life. Right now, from our perspective, we didn't get what we asked for. But, how do we know that our prayers weren't effective? We can't, until we stand in the presence of God and see how things really worked. What do I mean? I really don't know how God answered our prayers. Right now, from my limited perspective, it seems as though He did not respond. When I stand in His presence, and see things from His perspective I may see things differently and with a better understanding. At that time, I may realize God did answer our prayers for Ryan's life and he now not only has life, but life eternal because of our prayers. That is an awesome thought, isn't it?

So, in this chapter we have learned that God does hear

our prayers. He can and does respond to them, though sometimes those answers are not what or how we expected them, and that when we are forced to wait upon God, it says more about us than it does Him. With all that said, how should we pray, and what should we pray for, then?

I still believe that we should pray for anything we feel we need, and that means ANYTHING! We should be specific about what it is we desire and why we desire it (See Matthew 21:22 and Mark 11:24 for biblical evidence that supports my claim.)

This sounds contradictory to what I said earlier about not taking into account God's perspective, doesn't it? Well, I was getting there. From the two passages I stated previously, it is obvious that we are told to come to God. It is a privilege we have as children of God. We should take advantage of it. God knows our needs. When we pray, we are not telling Him something He doesn't know. Instead, we are telling Him that we are in complete dependence upon Him for everything and are looking for His perfect plan in any given situation. That is not a bad position to be in either.

Now, let's synthesize this all into a summary statement that we can take with us into our next prayer time. When we pray, there are no limits to what we can request (God is powerful enough to supply it), but as we determine what our request should be, we must truly seek after God's kingdom and righteousness (See Matthew 6:33). After our request has been offered, we must keep in mind that our petition does not obligate God to answer it exactly as stated, but that He will supply His best to us if we are willing to wait upon Him. Our reaction to His delay says little about Him and everything about us.

The bottom line is this, because we know our heavenly Father, we must trust that He will answer our needs by supplying what is best, even when there is delay or the answer is, "No". This thought gave us the energy and willingness for PRESSING

ON when we would have much rather PRESSED STOP. You should do the same.

(Some side thoughts: Are you really praying for something or for a situation you are in? Try something I did. I would write out my prayers, holding no feelings back. If I was angry, I communicated that. If I was confused, that was written. God knows how you are feeling, don't conceal it. Bear it before the God who loves you just as you are...even when angry or confused. Does He know you are human? Oh yeah, and He loves you still. By writing my prayers, I could see the progress in the situation, sometimes non-existent, otherwise. I could see where I had been, currently was, and make plans of where I would be. Finally, I could see how God was moving, and trust me, it seemed like He wasn't for three months as we watched Ryan progress through life.

Also, I do not want you to think that I am down-playing your situation by some of the comments I have made about prayer and your response to it. Instead, what I want to do is challenge you to pick your head up and take a different perspective about the whole thing. I know that you are in a sticky situation, but just as God saw us through ours, I am completely confident He will see you through yours. My request is that you give him the chance to work before you slam the door on Him. He will come through. Will it be exactly the way you planned? Most likely not, but are you willing to stick with Him anyway? My wife and I decided that we would rather have God on our side doing things His way, than not having Him at all, and letting us do them our way, something we had no control over anyway. Please, consider our thoughts, and do the same.)

chapter 4

Is God my co-pilot?

Occasionally, I've see a bumper sticker that reads. "God is my co-pilot." At first thought I'm comforted by that. To think that God is there beside me as I go down life's highway is refreshing. Whenever I need Him, He's never too far away.

I understand the message that the sticker is trying to convey. It IS good to know God is there. But, you know what? As I think about that sticker, something makes me wonder. Is God really my co-pilot? Let me say it another way. Am I really the pilot in control of the vehicle? Am I calling the shots? The one in charge? Am I in control?

The more I think about it, the less I believe that bumper sticker. If I'm completely honest, I'm never in control of things. Regardless of what I believe (or convince myself of) I am not in control. Someone (or something) else is.

That's the subject of this chapter. Who's in control? When things get hectic and we've lost it, does anybody have it together? How do you know one way or another? If God is in control, then why do things seem so out of control? If God is not in control, then WHO IS?

As we progress through this chapter, I need you to use your imagination. If you have to close your eyes for that to work, then occasionally put the book down and do so. Regardless, I need you to imagine that you're riding in a car. The good news is that God is in the passenger seat...as co-pilot. The bad news is that I'm driving. If you can overcome that thought, then we'll do okay.

Anyhow, we're driving on our way to an important meeting. I am in the driver's seat enjoying the control I have in deciding where we go, and how we get there. As back seat rider, you have no say in where we go. And, since God is only my co-pilot, as pilot, I have the ultimate say of what we'll be doing. He may give advice or direction, but I can override His input. That's the joy of being the "pilot," you know.

"Stop the dream, Leland!" I hear you saying. I get the feeling you're not liking this setup. Actually, maybe I'm not either. In fact, as I think about it, it's completely unrealistic. For the time being, I may be behind the wheel, but does that mean I am in total control? By no means. Does that mean that God is relegated to only an advisory role? By no means. Something has to change, but what?

With me as pilot and God as co-pilot, who does that put in charge? None other than ME! But, it's obvious in life that I am not in control. In fact, I shouldn't be driving.

Therefore, rather reluctantly, I get out of the driver's seat and allow God to take over. This is a big step for me, but I can handle it...as long as I'm still in the front seat! Things go smoothly for a while. I'm comfortable with how He's doing.

But, then, He doesn't turn where I wanted, or thought we should, so I reach over and grab the wheel and force the car into a sharp turn down a side road. You scream out, "Are you crazy, man? What's wrong with you? We were doing just fine!"

"I think we should've turned here so we can get where we're going," I respond.

"Yeah, but who's driving? You or Him?" Reality hits me. Inside I know that I had given God the wheel, but here I am taking back the controls. Why would I do that? Why should I do that?

I can't find a legitimate reason for my crass behavior, other than, maybe I still want to be in control. And, that's wrong! I realize my mistake, and turn to God and say, "You take us on the road You want to."

Again, things go well, and we travel for some time before any mishaps. God's doing a great job, and I see that He apparently knows the roads much better than I do.

But, then...something happens. I look at the clock on the dash and realize we are running behind schedule. We're going to be late! I ever so confidently say, "Uh, God, we're not quite on schedule. If you're going to get us there on time, you're going to have to speed up a little."

In the back seat I hear you clearing your throat. And, no, it isn't because you have something in it. Instead, you're trying to get my attention, and make a point. You don't have to say a word. I know what you're thinking just by the look on your face. After a quick thought of throwing you out of the car, I realize I messed up again.

Sure, I didn't stick my foot over there and press on the accelerator. But, again, I'm trying to take control, in a more subtle way this time. It still isn't right. After a few minutes of silence, I confess my mistake. Apparently I really don't trust God to get us where we're going correctly, safely, nor on time.

Somehow, I'm going to have to allow God to take control of the situation, and then trust Him completely through it all, even when I desire to be in control. How am I going to do this? For me, I'm going to have to get out of the front seat. So, as we travel down the road, I crawl over the seat and join you in the back.

Again, we travel down the road. This time, though, you and I strike up a conversation, and totally trust the Driver to transport us safely and quickly. Before we know it, we've arrived at our destination, and even on time!

God knew where He was taking us, how to get there, and got us there exactly when we should have.

What's this strange story tell us? Let me remind you, this chapter is about control. It's especially about who has it.

Our little story makes it obvious, if we're honest, that we are not in control, and shouldn't be if we could take control. There are some things we just can't stop, can't fix, and couldn't change even if we wanted to. What does that say? Someone else must be in control. And, who you think is, has a profound effect on how you handle life's ebbs and flows. Let me illustrate.

A while back I was reading in the newspaper where an 18 year old girl had died. That always gets me. So young, so much future, so sad an ending. Then when I heard the details of how she chose to die, my heart broke. How can a person (a young one, at that) get to the point where everything is so out of control that life isn't worth living? Instead of stepping up a notch, a person chooses giving up.

I don't know the girl, where she was from, if she ever heard of God, etc. It does help communicate my thoughts though. When things get out of control from our perspective, we humans, need the assurance that Someone has everything under control. Does it matter what I believe about Him being in control? I think this story points out that it does matter. When things are so out of control that you and I can't handle them, we can always have that assurance that God IS in control. Unless, of course, we don't really think He is capable of being in control.

Remember me in the car? That was my problem. Even though I "thought" God could handle it, when things didn't go as planned, my true beliefs came out. Ultimately, I wanted to have some control, and that's where the problems would occur. Until I sat back and let God handle the situation the way He wanted, I could not have the peace and assurance I needed to relax.

How does one get to that point where they can fully rely on

God and His control? I believe the first step is looking at Scripture and studying the sovereignty and control of God. If you don't have a firm foundation upon which to build your structure, it won't matter what materials you use, sooner or later, cracks will appear.

For the next few minutes I want to take you through a process of thought. Take your time. Work in and out of every nook and cranny I take you through so that when we come out the other side, you understand where you've been. If you have to read a paragraph more than once, don't worry about it. Do it! No one else will know.

The first thing I have to do is make a statement. It's sort of my "here's where we're at now" statement. It's where we'll start on our journey through this issue.

God is in control. He is completely and comprehensively sovereign. Nothing escapes His notice. Nothing gets to the point where He steps back and says, "Oops." Though things seem horribly out of balance (from our perspective), they are not out of God's hands and total control (God's perspective). Again, God is completely in control of all things. Charles Ryrie puts sovereignty this way:

> "The word means principal, chief, supreme. It speaks first of position (God is the chief Being in the universe), then of power (God is supreme in power in the universe) . . . A sovereign could be a dictator (God is not), or a sovereign could abdicate the use of his powers (God has not). Ultimately God is in complete control of all things, though He may choose to let certain events happen according to natural laws which He has ordained."[2]

In common language, what is he saying? God is above all creation in position and power. He does as He wishes, when He wishes, how He wishes. This could be bad, with a capital 'B' if God was not the God He is. Because He is loving, caring, etc. this attribute should give us comfort rather than cause fear. God, overseeing all things, and in control of all things, has the power to do all things. This includes allowing all things to happen. Nothing, and I mean to say, NOTHING, happens outside of God's watchful eye. Whether bad or good, pretty or ugly, sad or happy, God is in control of what takes place. That is what it means when I say God is sovereign and in control.

This bothers some people. If He is in control, why does He not do something to help my perspective? I will grant you, that's a good question. I have to answer honestly, I just don't know. I have some good ideas of why, but if I say them I'm afraid you will make them all-inclusive answers from God. In other words, you'll make me speak for God and immediately my credibility collapses. I can tell you this, though, and feel comfortable with it: just because things seem out of control to you (and me), it says nothing about whether God has lost control. Sometimes God moves in funny and weird ways. So weird that I just can't get it.

What you have to do though, regardless of what your feelings are telling you, is believe that God has things under control. Even if you can't understand quite where to go from there, start there. If that thought doesn't stick, even when it makes your head hurt, the rest of your journey may not matter.

Your belief that God is in control is the foundation to everything. Without a solid belief in God's control, your perspective changes. When you find yourself in a difficult time, how you react to it will be determined by your thoughts concerning God being in control and His ability to get you through that time. Without the conviction that God is there and in control, there is a danger of you giving up rather than pressing on. I don't want that to happen to you.

Some of you may be saying that I'm making this sound so

easy, almost flippant. "Just know God is in control and all will be fine." Trust me, that's not what I'm saying. Times are going to be confusing. Circumstances will make you wonder, even with God in control.

My wife and I were so confused (and to some point, still are) about why Ryan was not going to live. We were completely out of control. We could do NOTHING to get our circumstances in control. The only thing we could do was hold on to our belief that God was in control. And, that foundation was tested. The winds blew, shingles fell off, windows broke, boards popped and creaked. While the storm was upon us the one thing that kept us from giving up was that we believed God was in control. When the storm had passed we were thankful we had had that as our bedrock. If not for that, we could have been destroyed. And to be completely honest, I could have been that young lady I mentioned earlier. The potential was there. The confusion was there. The doubts about it being worth it were there. One more thing was there: the belief that God was in control. Because of that, and for no other reason, I am standing here today.

Throughout Scripture is evidence of God's sovereignty and control. We don't have to look far to see evidence that God is in control. One passage that I like is Ephesians 1, especially verses 11-12 where it says, "...having been predestined according to **His** purpose who works **all** things after the counsel of **His** will, to the end that we who were the first to hope in Christ should be to the praise of His glory." (Bold markings are mine)

What does verse 11 say to me? Two things:
- 1) ALL things work to fulfill His purpose, good and bad; and,
- 2) everything that takes place follows HIS will according to HIS counsel.

In other words, no one is giving God advice of how things should happen, and saying how they will be done. And, if someone is, God is no longer God. God alone determines all things and He alone determines what will or will not happen. Remember the "God is my co-pilot" bumper sticker? It isn't true. God is the pilot, the co-pilot, navigator, the whole crew. What are we? We are the passengers, so sit back and enjoy the ride. Nothing or no one will go beyond His control of the entire universe.

So, God being sovereign simply means that because He is God, the all-powerful God, He is in control. Nothing steps outside His plan, and nothing oversteps His authority.

What does this mean to you and me here on earth in the middle of these difficult times? They are not beyond God's control. Yes, they are bad—REAL BAD—but not so bad that they are beyond God's concern, or power to correct them. Does this mean He will fix them? Not necessarily so. That is where faith in Him to get you through comes in. The days may go on for weeks. The weeks may turn into months. The months into years. But, your belief that God is in control will be your one consolation that things will be okay in time (God's time).

But, if you're like me, you still wonder how this could be happening with God watching and not doing anything. Two things about that:

1) God is in control of everything that happens in His universe. Some things happen because of the directive will of God (i.e. He brings it to pass). Others happen because of His permissive will (He allows it to take place). Either way, they happen because of God's will. That's not the point of this comment. The point is that God is in control. I don't know which it is that takes place. Is it permissive or directive while it's happening? It doesn't matter while you are in it, does it? So I go to the next point.

2) We cannot tell why things are happening. In fact, to spend hours and hours questioning God about trials may have

little result. I'm not saying that to question God is wrong. In fact, if you aren't questioning God for something you aren't progressing spiritually. What I am saying is this, if all that matters to you is that God gives you an answer of why this or that happened to you, you may be horribly discouraged because there's no guarantee that He will ever answer your question.

Look at Job. He wrestles for 37 chapters with God and his friends in trying to determine why calamity had struck him. In the end, chapters 38-42, God talks to him but never mentions why. This may happen to you. It has happened to us. But, like Job, are you willing to say to God, "I know that Thou can do all things, and that no purpose of Yours can be thwarted"? In other words, "God, I have no idea what this is all about, but I trust in You because You are God and nothing you set out to do can be stopped (i.e. You are sovereign and in control.)" That's tough, I know, but it has got to be done.

For us, we still wrestle with why it happened. Why did our son die? Is it because of something we did? Or was God trying to teach us something? Let me quote Gretchen here:

> "Babies are all the time dying of genetic problems. We know the wages of sin is death (Romans 6:23), but maybe Ryan's death was not a direct result of something WE did, but an indirect result of sin in general. We question God—why did you let our baby die? Why didn't you do something? Do you think God is happy about the presence of sin in the world? It eventually sent His Son to the cross. He hadn't done anything wrong—the sin of everyone was upon Him. We are trying to do what is right, but we are not perfect. I believe He is pleased with us. I don't think He sent Ryan as a punishment to us, to make us hurt. We *may not* have had anything to learn from it. It may have just been a consequence of sin in general."

Why did I include this? To say this: we have no idea why Ryan had to die. We will probably never know what it was all about, at least during this life. BUT, we know that God is in control, and that since He is a loving God, He knows our pain and will one day make things right. No, He will make them perfect. If God was not in complete control, we could not say that, and we WOULD NOT press on, but would definitely press stop.

God is in control. If He isn't, who is? Nobody. And to me, to have no one in control is not comforting. I would rather God be in control and me not have a clue about what's going on than to know that no one is in control.

Here's another "car" story that may help. You and I are driving down the road, with me at the wheel. We are talking up a storm, enjoying each other's company. I am in control of the car as long as I have the wheel. All at once, in my excitement to stress a point I let go of the wheel (it could happen.) You are no longer comfortable with my control. In fact, you yell at me, tell me to stop the car because you want to get out. You'd rather walk home than ride with me! No one was in control, and it was not a comfortable feeling, was it? Some one needs to be in control, huh?

Now, go back to the first "car" story with you, me, and God. God was driving the car, remember? There came a time when I felt that He should've turned. I shouldn't have reacted by reaching over and grabbing the wheel like I did. Instead, I should've remained silent, and let Him drive on. We've got to learn to trust Him even when His actions may not make sense to us at the time. Sometimes we aren't happy with where God is taking us (Gret and I weren't), but because we trusted Him to get us through, we stayed in the car. Did we complain? Yes. Did we do some back seat driving? You better believe it. But, in the end, we decided that God knew the what and where and why of the situation and we could trust Him. Was it easy? Not at all. Will it be easy for you? Not at all. Must we do it? Yes. Will you do it? We pray you will.

Where have we been? We started out with the opening statement of "God is in control." We then looked at the thought of Him being sovereign. We thought a little about perspective, and how some situations look like they are out of control (to us), but to God, they are never that way. After that, we surveyed the fact that there will be times in this life where we may never truly understand what is going on, and God may not answer our every question. But, during those times, we must trust Him all the way. From there, we thought a little about how things would be without God in control. It occurred to us that if God isn't in control, then maybe no one is. That thought is unsettling, and possibly more nerve-wracking than God being in control. For us, even with the questions, we'd rather ride with the Lord in control, than not having anyone there. Finally, we stressed again the importance of trusting God during the ride. Even on the bumpy, twisting, and turning roads, stay in the car that God is driving. You'll not regret your decision.

And, now, we encourage you to press on. It won't be easy. The questions will still be there tomorrow, but keep riding with the Lord. He is capable and trustworthy. That knowledge of Him kept us PRESSING ON during those days when we would've much rather PRESSED STOP. You can do it, too, and you will!

chapter 5

"God is great, God is good . . . ?"

"God is great, God is good, let us thank Him for our food." A little child's prayer that most of us have prayed, or at least heard. But is it true? Is God really good? If He is, then why was our baby dying? If He was REALLY good, why was He not doing something to help Ryan? In the end, if He is so good, then why did He let our baby die? If God is good, why does evil exist?

I believe this question is at the center of everyone's mind. No, I don't mean for those who don't know God, but more so for those who do. "If He is so good, why didn't He do something when . . . ?" We've all asked that, or at least, thought it once in our life. If we haven't, we must be blind to, or ignorant of, the world around us. There is pain, suffering, aches, trials, dying, and on and on, all around us. How can we not notice it? It is a way of life, and we can't escape it. How can the goodness of God and all these bad things be reconciled?

In the next few pages I will attempt to help you make a little sense out of a very tough issue. As with the control of God, it will not be easy. It will take some deep thought on your part. As I say to those who know me, "this is a big, juicy steak, and you have no fork or knife." You are going to eat it anyway, even without the utensils. So, get your jaws loosened up and get ready to bite into it.

Before I start on the subject, I do want to say that the thoughts I have put down did not come easy. It took me several months to be able to say what I do, and even now there are times when I really wrestle with the issue. But deep down, I know that God is good. As you read these words, I know that you may not be able to say everything I do, as I do, but, don't discount them because of your situation. If you do, there's no point in going on. Many things do not matter if God is not good, and you must, at least partially, believe that. As the introduction to the book said, you are stepping into a journey that we have gone through (and still are). If you stop, it is no longer a journey, it is finished. Don't become the remains of those who did not keep going like we talked about. Take another step, wait a while, then take another. There is no time limit in your journey. Just keep progressing, that is all that matters.

Now, let's talk about the goodness of God.

When someone is asked about the goodness of God against the contrast of the evil in our world, they usually falter, stumble, then admit they cannot explain it. They then turn, doubting the issue themselves. Oh, not vocally or very seriously. But a part of them wonders, "What is the answer to that question?" Then, when trials come their way, the seed has been planted, and now being fertilized, it grows wildly. How can I say God is good when that bad thing happened? Again, there is no answer, and a little taller the plant gets. Over time, the weed overtakes them, and eventually it chokes any thought that God is really good, and their heart is turned from God because the question could not be answered. Trust me, the situations around that person WILL NOT point them to the goodness of God. Many times, because of the hurt and pain of the situation, a person is driven away from God, and not to Him. The world we live in will not testify in favor of God's goodness. It will do its best, and use any method possible to get us to doubt His goodness.

How do I plan on getting us through this part of the trek? Very carefully, believe me. First of all, I want to define what "good" means. Secondly, I will talk about why I believe God is good.

Finally, I will discuss what I believe reconciles the goodness of God and why bad things happen. Is this going to answer every question, from every angle? No. For centuries now, people have been trying to make sense out of this dilemma, and it hasn't happened yet. For our purposes, though, I want to at least help you get a better grasp of what it all means, and why it is important to believe that God is good, even with the presence of "evil."

WHAT *IS* GOOD?

At least, what does the "goodness of God" mean? For this I turn to A.W. Tozer, who puts it like this:

> "The goodness of God is that which disposes Him to be kind, cordial, benevolent, and full of good will toward men. He is tenderhearted and of quick sympathy, and His unfailing attitude toward all moral beings is open, frank, and friendly. By His nature He is inclined to bestow blessedness and He takes holy pleasure in the happiness of His people."[3]

That covers it. God, being good, means that we can trust Him to do what is right. He cares for us, and is tenderhearted and compassionate toward us. If ever there was a definition of "friend," it would be God. Who wouldn't want a person with the mentioned traits as a friend? His goodness is not easily understandable though. When we think of goodness, all we have to go on is human experience and example. God is that and more. In perfection, He is good. His goodness never fails, never fluctuates, and has never had nor ever will have a hinting of change. Those we know who are good, all have a bad day at some time where, for a moment, they are not good. God is not so. His goodness is perfect and eternal. It will always be there, because ultimately goodness is an attribute of God and because we know He cannot change, we know His goodness will not. He alone possesses perfect and eternal goodness, and He displays that goodness in a myriad of ways.

But, you're still asking, "Yeah, but what about this 'stuff' around me?" Let me get there. As always, I have to build a platform before I can speak, and that is what I am doing. You have to understand what God's goodness looks like before it means anything to you while in that 'stuff.'

WHERE DO I GET THE GOODNESS OF GOD?

Why do I believe He is good?

When I began the study of the goodness of God, I just believed it, without having one verse in mind which came out and said it. Once I got into it I realized, the thought that God is good is sprinkled throughout the pages of Scripture. Some of the verses actually say it many times.

Here are a few of the verses to give you an example of what I mean:

- 1 Chronicles 16:34—"O give thanks to the LORD, for He is **good**;..."
- Ps. 34:8—"O taste and see that the LORD is **good**;..."
- Ps. 100:5—"For the LORD is **good**"
- Ps. 106:1—"Oh give thanks to the LORD, for He is **good**..." Also, Ps. 107:1
- Ps. 118:1—"Give thanks to the LORD, for He is **good**;..." Also, Ps. 136:1
- Ps. 119:68—"You are good and do **good**;..."
- Ps 145:7—"They shall eagerly utter the memory of

- Your abundant **goodness**,"
- Ps 145:9—"The LORD is **good** to all,"
- Nahum 1:7—"The LORD is **good**, a stronghold in the day of trouble,"

(All bold text is mine.)

I think you have the idea. If one reads through Scripture and does not see that God is good, it is not the text's fault. The goodness of God is not only plainly stated, but is hinted at as you read through the accounts of the people He used within its pages. That God created the world, then said, "It is very good," hints at His goodness from the very first book right through to the return of Christ and the implementation of a perfect kingdom in the final book. The goodness of God cannot be overlooked.

Why do I believe that God is good? Because the Bible says so. Will the world *always* make it as obvious? Definitely not. In fact, it will (and does) cause us to wonder, but when we turn to the Bible, God's revelation of Himself to mankind, we realize that it is something God wanted us to *know* about Himself because it is stated so often. What is our response then when we wonder if God is good? The only response is to know that it is true. Not because everything we see or face is good, but because God has said that he is good and that's it.

Is this easy while in suffering? By no means. But, hold your thoughts for a little bit, because I plan on dealing with them in a moment.

IF GOD IS GOOD , WHY DO I HURT?

Now we get to the heart of this chapter. If God is *so good*, why am I suffering like this? For us, it was stated like this, "If God is *so good*, then why is Ryan suffering and not being healed?" You can change the question to fit your situation, but the question is still there. Throughout the process, we found it difficult to come out and say that God was good. If He was, we sure had a hard time seeing it. Deep down we still believed He was, we just couldn't say it. What were we going to do?

It ate at me for months. I was preparing for a life of ministry and service to a God Whom I could not say was good. There was no way I could go on with this, and I had to make some decisions. For months I wrestled with this issue. I wrestled with God. I wrestled with my thoughts. I wrestled with anything that would fight back.

Finally, one morning during my quiet time (which during the past few months had not been so quiet) something clicked. Thoughts rushed in on me that I had never had. They left my mind swirling, almost hurting. The rest of the day I was in another world, trying to truly comprehend my thoughts. Could this be it for me? Could this be the solution to my life-long problem of God's goodness amidst trials? (Notice I didn't say answer to my question. I still question why things happen, but not with the same perspective as before.)

Following are the thoughts of that morning, read them slowly, carefully, and repeatedly. Let them soak in.

"If God is good, then why does evil exist and bad things happen?" A good question, with a good answer!

God *is* good. God *is infinitely* good. Then what about the bad things? The events that take place around me (in a fallen world) are bad. There is very little good, true. But, is that evidence, I mean *real* evidence, against God's goodness? Does Ryan's situation really say, "God is bad!"?

Then if God is good, how can I see proof of it? Stop looking around you at this corrupt and dying world for evidence, and look beyond it. If Satan can cause you to doubt that goodness in God by overwhelming you with bad, do you think he will do it? Yes, and he's been doing quite well, don't you think? It is the common belief by the common public that God is not good because of bad events that take place. The score: Satan–1, us–0.

We must look beyond the present bad to that perfect good in the future that Christ has paid for and promised to us. Even as the world collapses around us, our thoughts must stay on the future where things will be good—no, they will be perfect. That includes my son, and yes, even me. That is the power that keeps me going when I, on my own, want to quit. That is the source of my joy even when events cause me deep and sincere unhappiness.

The goodness of God will not be easily seen in the events of the world around us. Does this mean he is not good? Should that cause us to doubt his goodness? I am sure you are answering "No" to both of these questions. But, then where do we go from here?

First off, you must realize the importance of the view of God that you have. If you have a low view of God, it will be difficult to nurture a reasonable view of Him by using evidence around you. In fact, you will never develop the view of God needed to sustain you through difficult times.

You must hold to a lofty view of God before you will have a lofty view of His goodness. That is where many have gone wrong today. Their view of God is so low and inaccurate that when difficulties arise, they cannot look to Him for guidance and strength because He is no bigger than they are. In fact, in many cases, *they* themselves *are* their god. To succeed, you cannot allow God to be displaced from the position He truly holds. In other words, a high and lofty view of God will bring life and its circumstances to higher and loftier positions as well.

Secondly, you must realize, again, that circumstances will not help you in the process. In fact, they will do all they can to discourage you from believing that God is truly good. At times, it will seem almost ludicrous to hold on to the belief that God is good. Do not let those times waver your belief in God.

Finally, faith will play an integral part in your ability to work through these times and questions. Faith is needed because you will be believing in something that, at times, will *not* be seen (the very definition of faith is believing in something unseen). Even when it is seen, it may not be seen clearly. Regardless, you must press on, believing that the God you believe in is good, and that the plan he has you involved in is good as well. Pressing stop solves nothing. So, don't touch that remote. Allow God to work His plan out. And, keep believing in Him to take care of you.

chapter

Is the church full of hypocrites?

How many times have we heard that? Too many. Is it true? By all means! The church is full of hypocrites, liars, deceivers, alcoholics, prostitutes, SINNERS—every one! Of which, I am one (and so are you). The church is full of people who talk one way and live another. They are mere pretenders of something much deeper and more significant than could ever be understood.

That is the mystery of *the church*. How can God take such a crazy, hodgepodge group of people and make them into a body which performs and operates on a spiritual level? That is beyond me.

After my comments in "Ryan's Story", are you surprised that I am saying all these negative things about the church? I am, so you can be too. I was expecting to start this chapter off with a completely different format. But, the truth came out before I could help it. The church has a long way to go before it reaches that plane God intends for it. It is full of people who can't find the true self they so desperately desire to find.

Does that surprise us? Should it? I don't think so. After all, who did Christ come for? The healthy or the sick?

Look at Luke 5:27-32 for a second. Jesus calls Levi, a *tax-collector,* to have a meal with Him. Once the party had begun,

Jesus was surrounded by the "scum of the earth" of the day. He was in the midst of hypocrites, drunks, thieves, crooks, and the likes. He was there willingly, talking with, working with, and loving them. The religious leaders reveal their coldness of heart by inquiring why he would associate with such a horrible group. After all, he was surrounded by some of the worst characters of the time, and on top of that, they were *sinners*! GASP and GULP!

Jesus responds, "You're right. I am keeping company with some pretty shady characters, some of which, I totally disagree with their lifestyle. But, tell me, who needs me worse, those who are well (or at least think they are) or the sick (and who know it)?"

He was making a statement. There are those who think they are healthy. At least, better than the guy next to them. For those, there is no medicine. They are sick and will not accept treatment. Their case is closed. In essence, they are as good as dead, just give them time.

There are others, though, who are incredibly sick and want help. Sure, they still have the fungus of the world all over them, and may even smell a little rough, but they know they are in trouble and are looking to be healed. Jesus came for *them*. He came for *you* and for *me*, if we admit that we are in need. If we don't, there is no use.

For us to claim that we are any better than the person beside us is a danger signal that we may be stepping over a fine line between one who can be helped and one who can't. The statement, "The church is full of hypocrites" is generally used by those who are as sick as the rest, but just won't admit it. For them, no response is needed. They are beyond human intervention. God will have to deal with them as He sees fit and for us to fret over their comment is pointless.

The church *is* full of hypocrites, true. But, is that a legitimate reason to reject God? Definitely not.

Now, on to the next step.

How *can* God take such a group and do anything with them? That is the mystery. Many of the people who helped us would admit they are hypocrites, but does that mean they are *all* wrong? Of course not. They know they are, but are taking the medicine needed to correct the illness. That is how God works through them. They are not perfect, but are willing to go under the care of the Master Physician and do what is prescribed by Him. Those who admit their need, and turn to God for the cure, become the Church. They are not perfect people, but recovering, and overcoming, sinners.

In Scripture, the church is explained as a body. We are all one, working together. When we mention the church as a body, we should realize that the pattern is not our body, but Christ's. We are "besieged by disease, subject to injury, destined to death and decay,"[4] and by using our bodies as the pattern taints the imagery God intends for His Body. Whenever Scripture uses the imagery of the church being a body, it is always stated as being Christ's body, of which, He is the Head. This helps explain the mystery a little. Let me go further with a story.

One day, while out working in the yard, I accidently cut my hand very badly. In fact, it needed immediate attention. What did I do? Naturally, I took my other hand and applied pressure to slow down the bleeding. I then got up and walked inside. I turned on the water, cleaned the wound, applied salve, dressed it, then went on. Every other day or so, I did those steps again as I cared for the wound until it was healed. Finally, it was just a scar, and needed no more attention. I went on with life.

Where is this going? Well, the hand that was hurt could do nothing without the rest of the body pitching in to help. Otherwise, I would have bled to death. Instead, my one hand reaches over to help, my feet carry me into the house, my eyes survey the situation, my mind determines what is needed, the other hand aids in the cleansing, my mouth blows gently to dry the area, and so on. It was a concerted effort on the whole body.

That is what God intends in His Body. When one goes down, the others pitch in to return the fallen one to normalcy. Pulling alongside one another, we fight on.

Is this the way it really is? Not always. Maybe the church has let you down before. Now you need help. Is the correct response to avoid them? Or should you step in and do what you know is the right thing? I know you know the answer, so I will stop there.

Either way, when tough times come, and they will, where can you turn? First, turn to the Savior. Tell Him your needs, your concerns. Spill your guts before Him. Then, turn to His Body, the Church, and ask them to help. If you can't turn to brothers and sisters in time of need, that is a terrible position to be in.

Now, before I leave this subject, I have some things to say to each side—the person needing help, and the church in the position to help.

First, if you are needing help, this is a tough position to be in, I understand. Can you go to them without being labeled? Will they accept me? Will I be expected to "pay them back" the rest of my life? Will my pride let me do this? On and on the questions can come. All of them are real, and the fear builds up. Even to the point where you choose not to go before them and ask for help. Please, God never intends for you to go through these times alone. Everyone needs someone sometime. That is a fact of life. Maybe it is now for you. Don't let those fears get the best of the situation. You never know what God is working out, or how he is planning on blessing and using you. By refusing to turn to others, a lot may be missed.

Second, if you are one not in the midst of problems, and one comes to you for help, please, be sensitive...to the person and to the Holy Spirit. They need you. By doing the things mentioned above, you may be thwarting the work of God in someone's life. Don't mess that up by being judgmental, insensitive, and proud. Your willingness to be used by God in this situation may change a person's life forever. Don't miss that chance.

Finally, it is time for the church to start fulfilling its purpose by reaching out to the people in need. The days are gone when they may turn to us. We must search for them, then rescue them from where they are. That will take a person who is paying attention to those around him. He must be focused on looking for opportunities, always listening for the cries of the hurting and perishing. Then, in offering that helping hand the person so desperately needs, someone is saved.

If we, as believers, in a church, can become those people, we will never be accused of being hypocrites again. Let's work to make that saying obsolete. That will take us being mindful of how we are living out our lives before others, especially while we are "out in the world." We are called to be those who offer hope and comfort to people who are hopeless and hurting. Too often in the midst of our "busyness" we walk right by people who need us (and the Lord).

People who are beacons of light in the midst of someone's valley, or salt in someone's tasteless world can work wonders. That is what happened to us. We needed others to be there and they were. They came out in droves. People who *really cared* for us. In their caring we found a God who *cares*. That's right: *God Cares*. And He cares *for you*. By them displaying their love toward us we were reminded that God cares for and loves us, too.

If you are in need, be willing to reach out *for* help. If you are "okay," be willing to reach out *to* help. That is what makes the Body function. Work hard at being the part God has called you to be. Strive to be healed, or to heal. Fill your role.

There will be days when God works through others and in those days their aid will be the only thing that keeps you going.

They will give you the energy to press on, when, you know, you'd much rather press stop.

chapter

7

How's the view from the cheap seats?

Do you ever feel like you just can't seem to see the whole game? Something is always in the way? No matter how hard you try to get a better angle, your perspective just doesn't change a whole lot? That is life, my friend. There are some things that no matter what you do, will never be totally in focus. There will always be something missing from your perspective.

That, again, is life. From our human perspective, some days are a total, massive, complete blank. Nothing makes sense anymore. Pressures are too much to bear. People just won't leave us alone. Problems won't pass us by. **Life's things are a complete mess!**

Do you ever feel like that? Good, you are "normal". (I know, you're thinking, "But, I don't want to be normal anymore! My life is **not** normal.")

Maybe it is. You just can't tell. Remember, we are about to start talking about perspective. Let's dive in.

In life, there are things that we, as humans, just can't explain. Maybe, in life, there are a *lot* of things that we cannot explain. It seems that we are always in a hole looking up and wondering why we can't see anything.

Or, to put it another way, I will use a baseball illustration:

As a child, did you ever go to a baseball field that had a

big wooden fence along the outfield? Did you ever try to catch the game for a "reduced price" by looking through a knothole? That was a lousy seat, wasn't it? That, indeed, was a "cheap seat."

The view stunk. It didn't matter how hard you tried, there were times that events of the game were a little outside your perspective and you had to guess at what was going on. Then, the ball returned into view and you could see what was taking place.

This story reminds me of life and my perspective of it all. I think I see the whole field and can make a judgment of what's going on, when in reality, I can see very little. In fact, I can only see a small portion of it all. My "knothole view" limits me so terribly that I have to learn to just wait for large moments (some seem like an eternity) until the ball comes back into sight.

How does all this work in life? Well, we have such a small view of what's really going on that it is destructive to get too excited until we can see the whole picture. Things are tough for you? Maybe it's the perspective. As soon as it comes into focus, you realize that it was actually something good happening. It just took time to unfold. Are you willing to keep watching the game though? Or would you rather back away from the fence and never find out what happened in the game?

That is a personal decision. You will have to decide for yourself whether you will stick it out, or give it up. But, let me help you with your decision by talking about some things that you should know before you make up your mind.

I can best start out this comment by saying one word: GOD. With God as a component, there is always a perspective to things that can change the whole equation. What seems hopeless to us, may be a walk in the park to Him. What seems insurmountable to us, is a small speck of dust to God. When we are ready to give up, God may just be getting started. If we give up, we may be missing an incredible event from God.

Perspective is everything. Sometimes, a different perspective can change a whole situation. Two people can see one accident from different angles and tell two different stories. It all depended upon their perspective. That is the way it is in life. We can see something happen in our life that makes no sense to us, but to God and His perspective it is making complete sense. It is all a matter of perspective.

With God involved, everything changes. One plus one always equals two in our world. But, if one of the "ones" is God, then everything changes. One plus one can equal ten. God changed the whole perspective.

Let me use a personal illustration to explain what I mean. While in the hospital, we had to make a decision about our son. We wanted to stop administering CPR (heroics) to keep our son alive. To do so, we had to go before an Ethics Committee at the hospital. As we explained our position, it became clear that they were operating in a 1+1=2 world. (Your boy has "x" plus "y" so that equals "z" and we feel such and such.) Then, we started adding God to the equation. For us, one plus one equaled five and we felt such and such. To make a long story short, they understood our method of addition and granted our request. It was not easy though.

God changed the whole perspective.

Now, shifting gears. I want to take this perspective thing to a different level. God can change the perspective, but there is more to it than that. We must remember that our perspective may not be God's. Let me explain, using the same baseball story as earlier.

You are on the outside looking in. You only get glimpses of the game. You cannot form a full thought because of your limited perspective. God, on the other hand, has the best seat in the house, maybe the press box. He can see the whole field, stands, etc. equally as well as at any point in the game. Because of His perspective, the game takes on a whole new meaning. Do you get the point?

When it boils down to it, we really have no idea of what things really mean, but God does. His perspective far exceeds ours. In fact, with God, the baseball analogy falls apart because God not only sees the game He is at, He sees every game in the whole world equally as well and with equal knowledge of the events of *every* game.

We must not forget this! During bad times, we so quickly get caught up in our perspective that we forget that God may have a different perspective in the whole thing. The Bible is full of examples of people who left God out of the equation. (See Daniel 5:1-31 for one of those.) To leave God out of the equation makes any perspective worse. There is something about adding God to things that makes the impossible possible.

And that is what we must keep in our minds during those difficult times.

We see that in Scripture. As the angel told Mary about what was going to happen with her, he added the comment that, "For nothing will be impossible with God." (Luke 1:37) It wasn't that Mary was going to have a child that was impossible. It was that she had never had sex with a man that made that impossible. She was pure. To have a baby would be impossible. But with God the whole thing changes.

Another instance of impossibilities is found in Matt 19:26. "And looking upon {them} Jesus said to them, "With men this is impossible, but with God all things are possible." Things insurmountable to us, are nothing to God. From our perspective the road is impassible. From God's, it may be just a Sunday drive. That doesn't make the road you're on any easier, but it does change the way you look at it. God is totally capable of making impossible things possible for those who are seeking His will and

His way.

    For a perfect example of how God changes everything we can travel to a hillside where several thousand people were tired and hungry and far from the closest grocery store. Jesus saw their need for food and told His disciples to feed them. Of course, there was "humanly" no way possible of doing such a thing. It would take close to a year's wages to cover that kind of bill. Even if they did have the money, where would they find *that* much food where they were? This was bad! No, this was impossible.

    But, it was a matter of perspective. To the disciples, they were facing an impossibility. They had the wrong perspective. Their perspective was one without God and His eternal power included. To Jesus, it was a matter of getting the people organized, taking what food they did have, and then passing it out.

    What's the point of all this? Jesus did not really expect them to feed the multitude by their own power, but He did expect them to realize that with God in the equation, they could do anything. In fact, because they didn't get it with one large feeding, he did it again shortly thereafter. Following that He gave them a quick quiz to see if they got it yet. (For these two accounts see Mark 6:33-44 and 8:1-21)

    What are you to see from all this? At least three things. First of all, God is not expecting you to make it through where you're at alone. He is expecting you to make it, but not without trusting Him along the way. Secondly, because you don't have what it is going to take to make it, give what you do have to Him and let Him work with it. The five loaves and two fish wouldn't have been enough to feed the twelve, but with God in the equation, it was more than enough to feed at least five thousand. What do you have that He can use? No matter how big or small, He can do *big* things with it. Finally, God is expecting you to have a different perspective on things. Where most would see 5,000 unsatisfiable and hungry people, you are to see an opportunity for God to work.

Perspective is everything though. And that must be played out through the situation you are in. We were there with our son, yet with the understanding of God and His perspective that we had, we were able to cope with those times. Without that perspective, we would have folded it up and gone home.

So, how do we change our perspective? Simply put, we have to etch deeply into our minds the presence of God. We must, regardless of circumstance, be confident that where we may be lost and confused, God *is not*. Quite the opposite. He sees the full picture, and knows the most intricate of details, especially those we couldn't see if we wanted to. This, my friend, involves trust. A belief that God is really there, that He sees the entire path you are currently in, and that He will see you through it all.

To go through life without an awareness of God's perfect perspective can cause great stress. It takes away the hope so needed by many in difficult times. It takes away the motivation to press on, and sure makes pressing stop an enticing option. But, don't. Why? Because you know better, that's why! You have the right perspective. One that includes a God who makes your impossibilities a reality! He can take your five loaves and two fish and get you through any situation you are in. And, you know what? He enjoys amazing His people. Why? Because He is an amazing God.

I would like to add one quick personal note here. There are many times in life when you will never see the full picture. Some things will not be totally revealed to you in this life. Some things will not make sense this side of heaven. Some things you will not see fully how God worked through them. To some, this is not okay. They demand to know. They drive themselves crazy trying to find out the answers to everything, when it may be better they not know. Be careful. Learn to "be content with what you have." After all, no matter what, "we confidently say, The LORD is my helper, I will not be afraid" and that, my friend, we KNOW!

chapter

The B-I-B-L-E, is that the Book for me...?

As I sit back in my chair and begin this chapter, I have more thoughts swirling around in my head than in any previous chapter. I'm not sure why this is. Maybe it's that I'm about to embark upon a dangerous trek. I'm not just giving a "book review" where I talk about some book that some author put together and whether I liked it or not.

No. This Book is different. This isn't your ordinary novel, or best selling fiction. It isn't a biography, autobiography, or reference work. It isn't a compilation of stories to warm your heart. It isn't an easy "1-2-3" self-help book that promises a better life in 30 days.

The Author didn't give an educated guess of how things operate in life based upon a survey of so many people, or clinical reviews that indicated trends or norms for people. This Author *knows* what He's talking about in an omniscient (big word for "knowing all"), all-powerful way. We may second guess His views, but in the end His way is always best.

This book is so different than any other ever written (or ever will be). This book is *life*. It holds the mysteries of everything in life. It stands completely and fully on its own. No other book can claim those traits. Sooner or later, other books will be outdated. Times will change and the principles they offer will not carry over.

The Bible is not so. Its principles are timeless. They cross generations, ages, centuries, millennia. A person today reading it sees the same God as one reading it a thousand years ago. And, that is the secret of this Book. Before I continue with that thought, let's dive into some other thoughts.

People today (and probably throughout history) have wrestled with what the Bible "is all about." They've attempted to read the Bible and it just didn't seem to do anything. Even more so, they left feeling more confused than before. Why is that? Why is this Book so hard, or at least perceived that way?

I may not have all the answers to those questions but I do have one I'd like to throw at you. Could it be that many times people go to the text of Scripture with too many ideas before they have read it? Maybe they have a preconceived idea or expectation that hinders them from truly seeing what is being said.

Let me explain with an illustration. Have you ever heard about a person with a reputation of being a difficult person to work with or around? The story on him is to watch out. You have never met the person, but people have warned you about him. Then, one day, you are required to go see him for something. The feelings of fear, apprehension, etc. creep into your mind. You think of other options, ideas, whatever that will get you out of seeing him, but nothing helps. You finally give in and "do whatcha gotta do."

You enter his presence prepared for the worst. Your expectations are low as you enter the room and see him sitting at his desk. He leans forward and invites you to have a seat, which you take because of your trembling knees. The meeting begins and you find him business-like, but cordial. You soon realize there is no need for the fear, etc. you had earlier.

Now stop the story. What does this have to do with the Bible? Could it be that as the person in the story was affected by preconceived ideas about the other, so we are bothered by preconceived ideas about the Bible?

This could be played out in a hundred different ways. It could indeed be a feeling of fear and apprehension as we enter the text that causes us to miss the point. It could also be inaccurate expectations of what the text is to say or do for us. Or, it could be misconceptions of what the Bible truly is.

Personally, the last two were brought home to me during our time with Ryan. I was guilty of both.

Concerning the first, I realized that I had inaccurate expectations of what the Bible was for. I had always believed it was some kind of "life's manual" that held all the answers to every problem one could ever face in life. There was nothing a person would ever confront that was not covered somewhere in its pages. It was a convenient booklet to have around when circumstances arose that could not be fixed.

A perfect example of this thought follows. You have purchased a new VCR and have it hooked up and ready. One thing, though. The clock is steadily flashing: 12:00–12:00–12:00. How can that be fixed? Go to the manual (the one you have not used yet because you don't need it). In the front pages is the Table of Contents. You find the page where "Setting the clock" is found. You follow the steps and presto, the clock is set to the desired time. The manual fixed it.

If the Bible is a "manual" for life, then we need to go to the Table of Contents or index and find the issue we are dealing with and all our problems will be fixed. You know what, though? That doesn't exist. There is no listing of problems with solutions in its pages. In fact, if you go to it for the solution to problems, you may leave frustrated more times than not.

Based upon that fact, the Bible must not be a "manual" for life alone. It is more, but what? Before I answer that, I want to talk about the second item above.

Maybe a lot of the problem with man and the Bible is the fact that we don't understand what it truly is. By not understanding its real purpose, we miss the point it's trying to make, and thus become frustrated with it and God.

To make this point more clear for you, let me share a story. As Gret and I progressed into the circumstances with Ryan we soon realized we were in deeper than we could ever handle. In fact, we were not staying afloat anymore. Very few things were making sense. Our conversations were no longer "just talk." Everything we said or thought revolved around what we should be doing with and for our son. Briefly put, we had no idea what we were doing or should be doing. We had a lot of questions that were not being answered. Where could we turn for help? We thought the Bible was that place. Being a seminary student and future pastor, I felt that I should dive into its pages and find the direction we needed.

I began poring over its pages looking up verses people had given me, verses I had heard, verses I had never seen before, and so on. I was bound and determined to find the answers to our problems and come out smelling like a rose and looking like a hero to those around me. I know this will be hard to believe, but that didn't happen. Something did happen, but not what I expected.

Every time I went to the text for answers I kept getting something else. It didn't matter how hard I tried to avoid it and find what *I* wanted, it kept showing up. Instead of realizing the answers, I kept catching a glimpse of God. I kept seeing more of Him, understanding more about Him, and getting to know Him a little more. It happened over and over and over. I would read its words, find no answer, but see a little more of God.

One day as I came to the text expecting to get answers I saw a different glimpse of God. At first I cried out to God for some answers. Then, it dawned on me. I had found my answers.

He was staring me right in the face. That's right. I had come to the "manual" looking for answers and had found that they were all answered in God. If I would merely trust Him, the questions I had would take on a new meaning, and the answers would come through Him.

My misconceptions of what the Bible truly is had caused me to overlook the one thing it's for. Simply put, the Bible is not just a manual. It was not written to reveal all the mysteries of life. It's not to answer our every question. What's it for then? **It is God's revelation of Himself to mankind.** In other words, it's how God wants man to see who He is, how He operates, and how we should respond to Him.

If you go to the text looking for something else, you may find it, but you will have missed its main point—the path to knowing God. Once I realized that I was to be looking for God in its pages, then and only then, did I start to get my answers. Things that once confused me started to make more sense because I was starting to see them through His eyes and with His heart. For us, that made everything change. Our questions were different. The way we asked them was different. And, gradually, we were different.

In the pages of Scripture, we had met God, face to face, and we had changed because of it. Our circumstances and difficulties were still there. The pain was still there. Some of the questions were still there. But, somehow, we had moved closer to our Living and Loving God, and that made everything better.

The Bible may not have had all the answers we *wanted* within its pages, but it did have what we *needed* more than the answers. Those glimpses of God and the ensuing relationship that was developed through those contacts have made a drastic impact on how we respond to problems we face today. In a few words, we will never be the same. And we're thankful for that.

When I enter the pages of Scripture now, there is a

different attitude. I still ask questions, and search for the answers. The difference is in how I look for them. Before I open its pages, I ask God to:

1) reveal to me what He wants me to know about Himself. I want Him to show me more of Himself, so I can understand Him better. The more I grow in my relationship with Him, the more I find the answers in life I'm searching for.

2) reveal the things hidden from me about the situations I am in. As I see Him, I start to see things I had never seen before about the people around me, the things I've faced, and the things I may be facing. It's as though there's a light illuminating things previously shadowed.

I'm starting to see and understand Psalm 119:105, where it says, "Your word is a lamp to my feet and a light to my path." I can see how some things have worked for me, and light has been shed upon things I just could not understand in my life. This light has made the things in life make a lot more sense. And, now, I find myself longing for the light and lamp the words of Scripture give me.

Now, before I go on, I must say something. It's sort of a disclaimer, yet not to protect Scripture (it can defend itself just fine without my help). All I want to say is that there have been times in my quest for answers where the passage(s) did not completely satisfy me when I first came to them. When I was done, I knew there had to be more. This just couldn't be "it". The tendency was to close the pages and give up because it didn't do anything for me. But, the more I stayed with it, and the more I read, the more I found. In fact, there have been times when that "incompleteness" has spurred me on to deeper and better things. It's as though the more I find, the more I long for from His Word. There is a deep hungering that I get when I read its pages. When I think about that, I'm reminded of Christ's words to Satan in the desert, "Man shall not live by bread alone, but by every word that proceeds from the mouth of God." As we begin to taste the sweetness of a relationship with God through the pages of Scripture, the natural follow should be a desire for more and more. We will only be fully satisfied by Him and His Word. We should strive for more, and we will as we spend more and more time with Him while visiting the pages of that "manual" called the Bible.

The point I don't want you to miss is this: "When at first you don't succeed, try...try again." There will be times when the pages seem lifeless, almost tasteless. Don't let that curb your desire for more. You must keep going back, sometimes, again and again, before the light finally makes it through. Giving up will not solve a thing. Those times when "nothing happens" are as much a part of the process of you knowing God as when "big things" happen. We cannot stop going back to the Source just because we didn't get some kind of "warm, fuzzy feeling" from Him the last time we were there. We must be willing to stick with it more than that if "big things" happen. In fact, as my mother always said (and I'm sure yours did too) "All good things take time and work."

The question is, "Are you willing to stick with it?" My hope and prayer is that you are and that because of your "stick-to-it-iveness" God will reward you (which I know He will).

Finally, I want to go back to the title of the chapter. That age old children's song--The B-I-B-L-E. Its words go like this:

> The B-i-b-l-e,
> Yes, that's the Book for me.
> I stand alone on the Word of God,
> The B-i-b-l-e.

I have learned from our situation that this simple song has more truth than I had ever given it credit for. It still amazes me how these childish songs hold some of the secrets of life, but as adults, we seem to get so "smart" that we forget all that we learned as children. If we would only retrieve and believe some of what we learned long ago, our lives would be so much simpler.

The third line of that song is the part I want to focus on right now. When life had knocked me down, and standing was impossible, I found the help I needed within the pages of the Bible. Since then I have learned that as long as my life is bathed within the pages of Scripture, I am more able to withstand what life has to offer me.

Why is this? I think there are at least two reasons for this. One, the Bible is not your ordinary Book. This Book not only has the secrets of life, it *is* life. Therefore, the Source of life will be found within its pages. Second, the strength you will find in its pages is because you have found that Source—the one and only, "...living and true God..." (1 Thess. 1:9). What He offers will be the grace and strength to keep you going in those times when you're running on empty and ready to quit.

I guess you could say that within the pages of Scripture you will find the God Who will cause you to PRESS ON, when you'd much rather PRESS STOP.

chapter

Does God *really* care about you?

Have you ever found yourself so bogged down with life that you can't seem to get off your knees? And when you do, something else just knocks you right back down? It comes for days, weeks, months, maybe years. Life just won't let you catch your breath long enough to let you unwind. You finally admit, "I quit! I can't go on! This is where it stops for me!"

This is a bad enough situation to find yourself in, but what if you've been praying for months for God to help you? What if you've been crying out to Him, and up to that point, he has flat out ignored you? The God who is always there, always aware, and always cares is none of the above. He is either non-existent, or too silent for your situation.

Those thoughts change everything. Why? Because for those of us who hold on to God for dear life need Him to be active in life's valleys. He is the first and last person we turn to. When He isn't there, what else is left? Nothing, and no one. We are all alone, abandoned, afraid, and dejected. We lose all hope. Somehow, we feel that God is not concerned for us.

In the middle of the valley, we cry out, "My God, my God, why have you forsaken me? . . I cry by day, but You do not answer; and by night, but I have no rest" (Psalm 22:1-2). Our prayers are empty echoes, and God seems to be nowhere in sight. This is confusing to us who know God. We know the promises He has made concerning His deep care and love for us, yet in the midst of difficult times it becomes very hard to see His movements.

So, with all that said, I have to ask the questions at hand: Does God really care about us? Does He indeed have that deep concern for us in those valleys? In the valleys, and during the silence, is something being said about God? Or do those times say anything about God at all?

It's difficult to know exactly what God is doing during those times because we can't see His movement (remember our discussion on perspective in an earlier chapter?). We can't feel Him holding us, caring for us. In fact, many times we feel completely abandoned by the God Who has told us to trust Him. Deep down, we know He is there, but what is He *doing*?

That's where it starts, but it quickly grows into: "Is He there at all? Does He really care? Has He left me completely?" Some may think those questions are ridiculous. God would never do that! And, they're right, but in the midst of the valley, it becomes much more difficult to say it that dogmatically. Look through the Psalms, and you will see David talking like that. What am I saying? People will criticize some for "even thinking" those thoughts, but the incredible David did the same exact thing. He had valleys. He had doubts. He had questions.

We can see those times in his psalms of lament. In the midst of trouble David calls out to God, but hears no response. He questions God's closeness, maybe even His existence. He struggles with it all. He knows in his heart God is there, but experientially, it just doesn't seem like it. And, that's where the confusion begins.

Face it, as humans, everything we digest is based upon experience. If we can't see it, hear it, feel it, we have a hard time believing it. That's not a slam, just the truth. The tension begins when you place a God in the picture who doesn't always operate within those boundaries. He isn't always touchable. He isn't always seen. He isn't always heard. Yet, He is always working and is always there. His operations go to another dimension within which we don't operate effectively. What is that dimension? Faith.

"Now faith is the assurance of things hoped for, the conviction of things not seen" (or heard, or felt), Hebrews 11:1 tells us. Three thoughts need to be looked at before we move on.

First, "assurance." Faith is the *assurance*, (that deep down belief that tells us it is true), "God is there and is working for me." Events occur, circumstances change, but that assurance stands. In our heart of hearts, we *know* God is working on our case, and is doing whatever is needed done. That assurance causes us to keep going on, even when experientially we are thinking about giving up.

Secondly, "conviction." Faith is no "warm, fuzzy feel good" emotion that carries us through troublous times. If it was only that, it wouldn't be enough to get us through because for many out there struggling along, the warm, fuzzy stuff ended a long time ago. We've gone deeper than that. Our emotions failed us, and now we are left in a position where we need more than that.

And, that is where faith steps in. It is "the *conviction*..." As I think about that word, I think of something that goes so deep within ourselves that it can't be touched by exterior environment. It's the "guts" of what we're all about. While everything else changes around us, our convictions remain...unmovable and unhindered. Our convictions are the nitty-gritty things that cause us to stand up and fight when our emotions, our physical abilities, etc. are saying, "Sit down."

Before we go to the third word, I must say this: To function properly in this fallen world, we will need both assurance and conviction. Hold that thought. We'll come back to it.

Finally, "not seen." Faith is built upon everything "not seen." Tension sets in. I want things I can see and handle. This stuff I can't see confuses me. It's hard to grasp it, therefore, I struggle with it. And, honestly, that's okay.

"Whew," you may be thinking. "I thought there was something wrong with me." No, my friend, nothing's wrong with you. It's quite the opposite. Everything is right with you. If you didn't have that tension, then something is wrong. Something is missing.

That is what's amazing about faith. It's not stagnant and lifeless. It grows and stretches as you grow and stretch in your daily life. It is fluid, always deeper and stronger with everything that you encounter. The thing is, though, at its deepest point, your faith must have some assurance and a few convictions to truly stand. There must be some deep down thoughts on which you can hang life's difficulties upon. Thoughts that help you make sense out of what you are going through and how it all works in the big picture of you and your life.

And, that is what I meant when I said earlier, "we will need both assurance and conviction" to make it in this world. Your world. Faith is the assurance of things hoped for and the conviction of things not seen. To keep going where you may be will take faith that has those two components. Don't try to go on without them. A faith without them is a shallow faith and may not get you through.

Now, before we leave this thought of faith, one more comment must be made. Faith is not enough. In fact, faith is not the secret. Instead, the secret is what you have your faith *in*. If you cannot be assured about nor have convictions upon that which your faith is resting, then you have nothing. For instance, you can have all the faith in the world that I will send you a million bucks for buying and reading this book, but it "ain't gonna get you nowhere." What you have your faith resting upon is what matters, not how much you have. Faith **is** important, and I don't want to downplay your need for it, but where you have it shadows how much you have.

Your faith in *God* gives you the reason to have the assurance and convictions you will need to make it through the valleys you will face in life. And, the convictions you have about God will determine how much assurance and faith you will have. If you are not totally convinced that God does indeed care for you, then there will be cracks upon which the winds of life can blow, bend, and break your structure. You must believe that He does, or there is no point in putting any faith in Him. If He can't be trusted for one thing, should He be trusted for anything?

This is where you must make a decision. What exactly do you believe when it comes to God's apparent silence in the valleys? Do you truly believe He cares, or not? The answer to those questions determine whether you should go on with God or without Him.

All I'm saying is that you must hold to your convictions that God does care for you. You must believe the promises He has given to you about "never leaving nor forsaking you" and that "He cares for you" (Hebrews 13:5 and 1 Peter 5:7).

We've just answered the question raised earlier "Does God really care for us?" with a resounding "YES!" Take that and bank on it. Set your anchor deeply into Him and hold on for dear life. He can and will take it.

The question comes up though, "During those times of silence, is something being said about God?" And, if it is, what is being said? This shouldn't take as long, even though it may be the tougher of the questions being raised.

First of all, it's really difficult to tell exactly what's being said about God during those times. Why? Because, during those times it's difficult to say anything about...well, anything. I have found that it's really tough to make a good judgement call during those times because of several reasons. Here are a few:

1) We are not emotionally ready or able to actually see what is going on. We are so caught up in the heat of the moment that everything that is stable within us is in total chaos. As a result, we have yet to truly understand something until we are standing on the other side of the problem. Then, things make a whole lot more sense.

2) We can't see the big picture while in the forest. Some people will say, "You can't see the forest for the trees" and they're right. We may very well be involved in a beautiful thing, but right now, the vines, brush, and trees of life have us so distracted that we can't see anything. Therefore, I have found it is better to hold judgement until we get out of the trees and can then see the forest. Never judge the valley until you're on the mountaintop looking into it. It will look completely different!

3) We are too damaged to see the real picture. The pain, struggles, etc. have got us down so far that we just can't focus on what really may be going on. As a result, we are just not able to make sense out of it. Months, or maybe, even years later when we have been healed, then and only then, do we start to make sense out of it all.

I think those three can get you thinking about that, and you can go from here. You know, though, throughout Scripture there is situation after situation, person after person, who was in a valley and couldn't see out. But, then in retrospect, they began to see what God was doing for them, and ended up praising Him for that valley. You can do the same, if you just keep moving. (Joseph in Egypt, Gen. 39-45, is a perfect example)

So, what do those valleys say about God? Very little, possibly. When God doesn't seem to work as we want, why do we start complaining to and about Him? Seriously, why is the natural follow to blame God when things are going bad? Do the valleys really prove God isn't involved with you anymore? Is God really to blame for the valleys? Let me share some thoughts I had during a class in seminary that involved this very subject:

> "God is so involved with this world and my life that to say He is "sitting on His hands" is borderline heresy. When it seems that He is inactive in my life it is a matter of perspective rather than inactivity. If a sparrow can't fall without His noticing it, could I encounter anything without Him being active in it? Then, it should follow that I could never say that God is not in control of what's happening, is not concerned about those situations, or refuses to be working in those circumstances, without in some form saying that I don't believe in God. Those statements, for sure, reveal nothing about God, but rather everything about my view of, and my faith in Him. If Joseph (and Paul) could see God working while sitting in a prison dungeon, how can I say He is not in the midst of Ryan's life? I realize now, I can't, and won't. I know you well enough, O God, to know that you are involved and do care about me and this valley I am in. Thank you."

With those thoughts, I have to mention too, that God has a way of stepping into your life and leaving you dumbfounded. The question is, will you ignore His work, or respond to it? To act or even think that God is not an important part of your life (if not *the* most important) is a dangerous position of ignorance.

Finally, for those reading this book, I need to offer some encouragement. Again, it is totally normal to be thinking that maybe God has in some way abandoned you. If someone has never felt that, then either they have never lived life, or they are in denial. We all have that tension in the midst of life of how God works through it all.

And, I want to go back to the psalms of lament mentioned

earlier to help you through those times when the tension is highest. Through those psalms, we can get some direction.

To do so, take a look at Psalm 13. There is a progression David goes through that we cannot overlook.[5] It looks like this:

1. An inward look. A look at where you are internally, and the tension that you may be feeling about how God may have abandoned you. See verses 1-2. This stage deals with how you are feeling inside yourself...that tension between God's care and apparent abandonment, etc.

2. There is an outward look. You look around and see what all is happening and wonder, "Is this it? Am I going to make it? Unless you help, God, I am finished." See verses 3-4. In the midst of the valley and all its darkness, you cry out because you are totally lost!

3. There is an upward look. You look up to God and in the midst of the valley, you remember how He has worked before, the promises He has made, and there is a peace (even for a moment) that He will work this time. See verses 5-6. Still in the valley, you find comfort from Him, and somehow through it all, you press on. Those times are strange because during those times is when God seems closest and yet farthest away at the same time. For the life of me, I can't explain it either. I do know that I've come to depend on them though.

Let's make it personal. The circle started with you on your knees, about to give up, crying out to God because you felt abandoned by Him. Then, you looked around and saw what you were up against, and cried out to God for an answer. A specific answer. Then, in full progression, you were convinced that God would indeed work for you and you cry out praises for what He will be doing based upon your "assurance and convictions" about Him.

As you progress through your life's event(s), you must not stop at step one or two, without continuing on to number three, for if you do, your chances of quitting right there are terribly high. You *must* recall, and re-affirm those convictions you have about God and his care for you, even when it seems that He has forgotten you, turned from you, or abandoned you.

God does care for you...deeply. He has promised that He will always be there, and we must believe Him. We must hold those thoughts tightly within our heart as we continue through the dark valley we find ourselves in. Sure, we will wonder. We will question. We will call out as though He isn't there, but deep down we must know He is and trust Him to see us through. We must trust Him enough to offer Him thanks and praise, even while in the midst of it all. If you look in, look out, and forget to look up, you are doomed.

That three step process was an integral part of our pressing on when we wanted to press stop. We knew God was there, and we stuck with it and now can look back and more clearly see the forest, and the wonderful scenery He brought us through. Don't give up! On life or Him.

Before I close, I want to share with you a psalm of lament that a friend from seminary wrote for us. As we progressed through Ryan's life, a man, Chad C. Clements was there for me so many times as a friend and a counselor. (I still have a stick-note in my Bible that he gave me that listed steps in the grieving process. I have gone to it many times.) The poem's title is:

Ryan's Psalm–A Psalm of Lament Over the Death of Ryan.

Oh my God, and my Creator You have deceived me!
You have misled me to think You care.
How could You fail in your creation when You are the "Great Creator?"
Do you not remember the rejoicing that we had at the conception of Ryan?
Does it slip Your mind how we pleaded with sincere hearts that You bring blessings to him and his mother?
I remember praying to You and praising Your name for what You gave!
I did my part why didn't You?
Are You not the God that is recorded in the Scriptures that declares what you create is good?
Have You, oh my God, made a mistake?
Did You fail in making Ryan whole?
You gave me great peace that You are God and I must trust you, but God Why?
Why have You given life to someone when You planned on taking it back so quickly?
Do You not care about the hurt and uncertainty?
What about Ryan's pain and torment?
Do You recall what it is like for his mother and father never to be able to have him kiss them?
Do You know what it is like to never see a child walk and run on his own strength?
Why then God should I rejoice in what You have done to us?
Yet, You have taken the time to bless us with his presence even for one hundred days.
You gave, and have taken according to Your will.
You have prevented the long term agony of his health by taking him to You.
I forget that it is Your presence I long to be in today.
I remember that You are a better Father than me.
I forget the privilege that Ryan has of seeing You first, rather than me and my years.
Forgive me God, I forgot that I will see Ryan again!
You have answered our prayers and it is me that is doubting, for You have not changed.
It is my feelings that wrestle me in torment because I forgot who You are, and how much You care.
We will again praise Your name because You are the "Great Creator!"
You have not failed us, but have done what is right for all of us!

And, with that, I will close this chapter. Always remember and be convicted about God's deep care for you. He is there, and will not let you down, regardless of what your senses, emotions, feelings, etc. tell you. Friend, press on with Him.

chapter

10

What's the point of it all?

We've come a long way since that night. You've seen us go through one of the most troubling times of our lives, and hopefully something we never have to face again. Right now as I'm writing this, it's almost four years since that December evening when this story started. Yes, four years. What could that say to you?

First, only time will heal some things. There will be circumstances in life that only as the years go by can you "get over them." Time seems to ease the pain. I'm so thankful to God who has given us the ability to "forget" a lot of the painful things of the past. Sure, they still hurt, but a lot of the little things that caused the pain have been lost.

Secondly, if you're right in the middle of something, be patient. Don't jump to any conclusions of where you're at. That would be a huge mistake that could cost you more than the situation you're already in. Give it time to unfold before you want to give it up.

Thirdly, even after time goes by, some things will never make sense. We're still not "getting" some of what we went through. What must we do? This may sound odd, but, the simple answer is, "Get over it, and live on." We've made the choice that life goes on, even if *we* decide to stop. Therefore, we're going to go on living. We hope you do the same.

As I think about where we've been, I wanted to leave you with some kind of impressive conclusion that would make everything come together. I don't want to "review." You can do that by re-reading the book.

Instead, I would like to close with some things we learned as we traveled along this incredible journey. The only reason for including them is to help you with perspective...a better perspective of where you are in your journey.

- We must always depend on God to know that He knows what He's doing even though we may not see the purpose in it.

- We must believe in His perfect timing and that our God is a Sovereign God and though His plan may not fit ours, His is best to follow.

- We must believe and hold tightly to our belief that God deeply loves His children, and cares for them.

- We must believe that our God is actively and intricately involved in humanity (your life) and can and does perform miracles.

- We must realize that if we depend on our own strength and energy, we cannot make it. We must realize that it all comes from God.

- There is a tension within us caused by God's knowing and our not knowing that, left unchecked, will eat at the very depths of our soul.

- As we progress through life, it will become evident that life is unfair. But, somehow, someway, God will make it all right in the end because He is fair.

- Sometimes you will shake your *head*, and say, "I don't understand!" Other times, you will shake your *fist* and say, "I don't understand!" God is big enough to take what you're feeling. Share it with him.

- We're all involved in a journey. God is with us throughout that journey, but that doesn't necessarily mean everything will be easy. Rather, we've come to say that our journey is *paved*, but steep, which is better than unpaved *and* steep.

- Overcoming difficult times takes more than "guts," it takes a mind-set. A mind-set focused and founded on an all-powerful God Who will bring you through.

This list is not exhaustive of the things we've learned. You've seen many of those lessons within the pages of the book, others we just can't put into words. Some, we're still trying to learn, and understand.

Another item I must bring up before we leave you is this: through it all, you must spend time with God. Search Him out, pray to Him, talk with Him, wrestle with Him. Truly strive to find out His view of it all. Too often, if He doesn't answer right away, we walk away. This is terrible. Give Him time. How long? Until He answers.

Why do I say this? I struggled for months how this whole thing of Ryan fit in life, especially, **my life**! I wrestled with God for some kind of answer. I wanted more than I was getting, and I wouldn't let go of Him until I got it. I waited and waited. Little things came up, but the big question was still there, unanswered.

Then, one night, through a dream, the tension was reconciled. Here is the dream: (Please understand, this is only a dream. I would never want to imply that I've found some new revelation, or make it more than it really is. Nor, am I stating that God will give you a dream that "speaks" to you. I'm only including it because I think it may help you make sense of things in your life.)

    I find myself driving in a car, going through a horrible fog. Landmarks, road signs, everything is concealed. I cannot for the life of me figure out where I am. After traveling for a while, completely lost, I pull to the side of the road and take out my map. There ahead, in the lights of my car, is a road sign with a number on it. As I search for it on my map, it's as though the map I'm looking at is for another state. It's as if I'm in Oklahoma looking at a Kansas map. It's completely pointless. In frustration, I pull back onto the road, completely clueless of where I am or where I'm going. I travel along, stopping every few miles trying to figure it out. But, to no avail.

    This goes on for some time, with me lost the whole time. I am tired, frustrated, and lost. Then, the image changes. I'm walking, still lost in an unmanageable fog. I walk along, stopping every now and then trying to make sense of it all. Again, to no avail.

    All of a sudden, as though walking through a wall, I come into the sunshine. The fog is gone. I look down at my body. I am bloody. My clothes are a mess. Sleeves are missing. One shoe is gone. My face is caked with dirt.

    I look ahead, and there on a throne, is God. He is saying something to me. I get close enough to hear Him, and he says, "You made it." It isn't surprise or shock. It is an, "I knew you would and have been watching you along the way" tone of voice, as though He was expecting me.

    I respond to Him, "Yeah, but look at me. I'm a mess. I'm all bloody and beat up. I didn't do a good job at it."

"That doesn't matter. You made it, that's what matters," He tells me.

After a pause, curiosity gets me, "What was that all about?" I ask as I point back over my shoulder to the storm I had just exited. There is another pause.

"That's what it was all about!" He responds as He points past me, a smile changing His face.

I look back, and coming out of the fog, one-by-one, is my mom and dad, my wife, my son, a few friends from my hometown, friends from seminary, and other members of my family. "Yeah, but what's that mean?" I ask.

"Leland, they were following you. Every time you stopped, they stopped. When you would go on, they would go on. Because you made it, they made it. That's what it was all about. You were my leader, and I'm proud of you."

At that point, I awoke. The dream crushed me, and healed me, all at once. It crushed me because I remembered all the times I felt like quitting, and could have so easily. The thought of how many people would've been affected by my quitting overwhelmed me.

It healed me, as well, as I thought about His words, "I'm proud of you." Even though I had at times thought He wasn't concerned, I now realized He was and had taken notice of my labors. That made it all worthwhile to know that I had been His faithful servant, even if I didn't know it as I went through it.

How can I make this dream make sense for you? Let me start with this. We all have a finish line to cross in life. It's out there, even when we don't see it. God is expecting us to cross it. Quitting is not an option. Finishing is all we can do.

That dream showed me several things. First, there was a line (and still is) that I am to cross. Secondly, I am not being timed. The goal is just to finish, not how fast I do it. God will not be more or less impressed with me because of my time. Thirdly, some of us will run across the line, completely unharmed and clean. Some will barely make it. We'll have scars from life, be missing clothes, legs, etc., barely dragging ourselves across the line. That's not the point. God will not dock His children for being dirty from life, or reward us for staying clean. The point is that we made it. And, finally, the response from God when we cross the line is always the same for everybody. He will be so happy to see you, me, and all His other children making it, and none will take precedence over others. His loving welcome is the same for all. He's just glad to see us, regardless of who we are and how we come across the line.

That to me is so comforting. The whole time I thought I was failing God by stopping along the way, getting dirty from it, and wanting to quit. But, in reality, as long as I came across the line He was completely happy with me. Getting there faster wouldn't have made Him love me more. Taking longer wouldn't have made Him love me less.

Don't miss that. If you have to, read it again. All God expects from you is that you stick with it. Tripping, falling, getting hurt along the way, are just part of the journey. He isn't giving style points, only faithful points. What does He want from you? He wants you to press on, even when everything and everyone around you is yelling out to press stop. Don't listen!

What's the point of it all? Life is tough. Winds will blow, storms will come. Things will hurt you. People will cut you. You will get lost. You'll want to give up. You'll fall down along the way. The days will drag on in a sickening echo one after another. Giving up will be so easy. You'll even think about it. But, somehow, you'll keep going.

Then, one day, you'll walk out of the fog, and there will be God, smiling and happy to see you. His arms will be open and ready to pull you close to Himself. He will comfort you, clean you up, heal your wounds, dry your tears, and put that smile back on your face that life took away.

You know what? All of a sudden, the things of life won't matter anymore. All that matters then is that you are in the presence of the God Who has brought you through it all, and that's enough. The "stuff" of life that caused so much pain is gone. Your heart is free, and it was all worth it.

That's the point. I am thoroughly convinced that God is able to make everything (including the death of a son, cancer, AIDS, whatever) all worthwhile when we stand in His presence and *know* that He has accepted us as His child. This sounds so simplistic and may even cause some to think I'm copping out, but it's the truth. That is all that matters to me, knowing that I am known by God.

I still have questions, but knowing God changes the way I ask them. I still have aches and pains, but knowing God soothes the hurt. I still grieve the death of my son, but knowing God gives me hope in that grief.

Do you see the point? Knowing and trusting in God changes everything. With God, we have Someone to turn to and hold on to that otherwise wouldn't be there. Also, with God, we not only have someone, we have *the* One who can get us through it.

Friends, we realize you may be going through some tough times, and our hearts go out to you. But, whatever you do, however you do it, **do not press stop**! Keep pressing on.

AFTER THOUGHT

It's hard to believe so much time has passed since Ryan was here. Our lives have changed so much. We now live in South Dakota, where I am serving as an Associate Pastor. The past few years have taught us so much, and things haven't been so easy as a pastor. But, God has never let us down.

On March 28th, 2000, God saw fit to give us a third child, Carissa Lynette. She is beautiful (of course), growing so fast, and yes, perfectly healthy. We can take no credit for her, and our praises go eternally to our loving, gracious, and caring Father above.

Finally, we want you to know that we appreciate you reading our book. It was good for us, as we discussed the things God brought us through. But, our intent was not therapy for us, but to help you along your journey. Our prayer is that the stories within its pages have done that, and you can see your life from a different perspective. And, as always, keep pressing on.

Notes

1. R. A. Torrey, *How To Pray* (Ulrichsville: Barbour and Company, Inc., 1989) p.22.

2. Charles Ryrie, *Basic Theology* (Wheaton: Victor Books, 1986) p. 43.

3. A. W. Tozer, *The Knowledge of the Holy* (San Fransisco: Harper and Row, 1961) p. 82.

4. Robert Shannon, *The New Testament Church* (Cincinnati: The Standard Publishing Company, 1964)

5. Ronald B. Allen, *And I Will Praise Him* (Nashville: Thomas Nelson Publishers, 1992) p. 150.